John Beeby

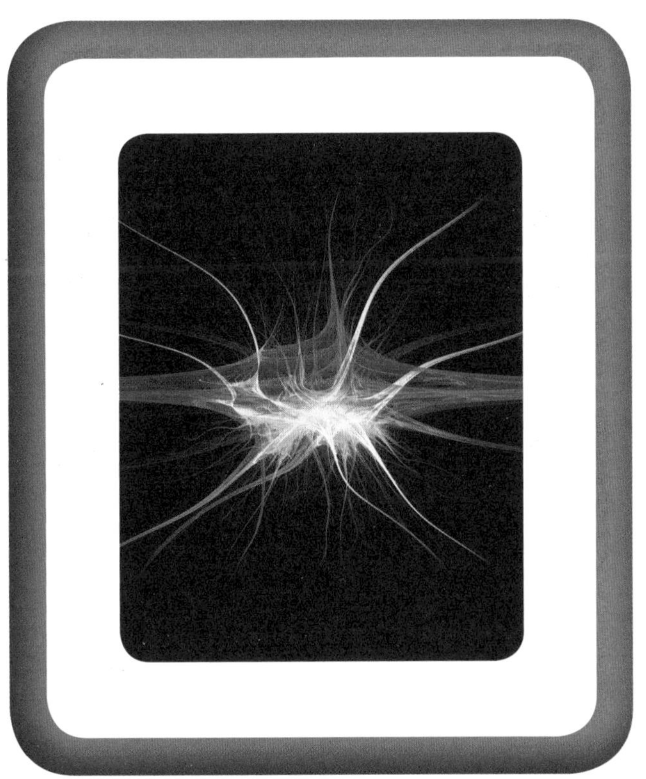

ESSENTIALS

OCR

GCSE Additional Applied Science

Revision Guide

Contents

Contents

Revised

Unit A191 – Science in Society

Unit A192 – Science of Materials and Production

A1 Sport and Fitness

Sports and Fitness Organisations

Sports, fitness and lifestyle facilities, e.g. football clubs and health clubs, use qualified **practitioners** to deliver their services.

Sports and fitness practitioners include...
- sports coaches
- personal trainers.

A **sports coach** helps people to reach their full sporting potential by...
- analysing their performance
- giving instruction in skills
- creating the right conditions for the person's development
- providing guidance, encouragement and motivation.

A **personal trainer**...
- designs a one-to-one programme to help people improve their health and fitness
- sets realistic personal goals
- helps the client with the use of equipment and workouts in personal training sessions
- monitors and records the person's progress
- gives advice about lifestyle.

Practitioners working in sport and fitness may require a sports science qualification. This could be a qualification approved by the Register of Exercise Professionals. They must be familiar with health and safety regulations, and the impact these have on their work, for example...
- preventing injury during exercise programmes
- dealing with injuries and first aid
- checking gym equipment for safety.

Lifestyle

Your **lifestyle** is your way of living.

Our lifestyle affects our health and fitness.

- excess **food and drink** lead to us putting on weight
- drinking alcohol and smoking tobacco will affect our health
- moderate **exercise** improves the strength and efficiency of our muscle, including our heart muscles
- **stress** affects our eating and sleeping patterns. When under stress, we feel tired and our muscles are tense.

Key Words Practitioner • Lifestyle

Health and Fitness

Your **health** is your physical and mental well-being and whether you have a disease or injury.

Our health is affected by:

- medication
- previous medical treatment we've had, previous injuries, operations and pregnancies.

Your **fitness** refers to your physical condition.

Fitness can be improved by exercise and proper nutrition. Fitness includes aerobic fitness, stamina and strength.

Baseline Assessment

Any sport or fitness programme starts with initial testing called **baseline assessment**.

Information collected in a baseline assessment includes…

- **gender** – men and women differ physiologically so calculations will be made according to your gender
- **age** – as your body gets older it becomes slower at carrying out certain processes
- **aerobic fitness** – your body's ability to continue working for long periods. Your recovery rate (how long it takes your heart rate to return to normal after exercise) indicates your aerobic fitness
- **body mass index (BMI)** – calculated from your height and mass using the following formula:

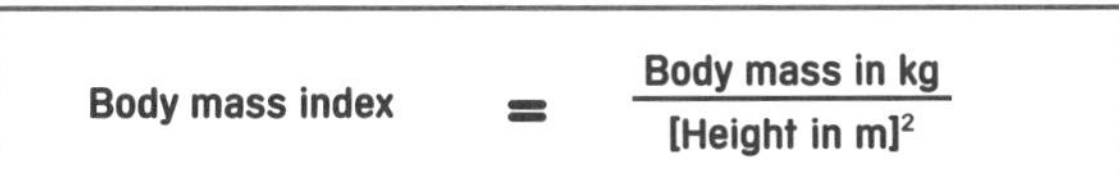

$$\text{Body mass index} = \frac{\text{Body mass in kg}}{[\text{Height in m}]^2}$$

A healthy BMI is between 18.5 and 25.

A body mass graph can be used to quickly identify whether you are a healthy weight.

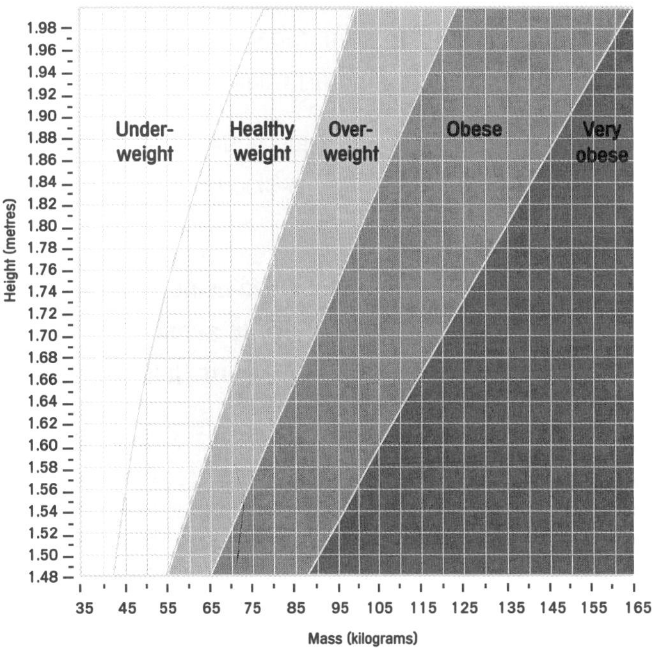

HT A client must be properly assessed before beginning a fitness programme. This health and fitness check includes questions about lifestyle and a range of tests. These tests may carry some risks to someone who is unhealthy. Any risks to the client must be assessed before tests begin.

Key Words Health • Fitness • Baseline assessment • Body mass index (BMI)

A1 Sport and Fitness

Testing Health and Fitness

Your **pulse rate**, **blood pressure** and **temperature** will also be taken as part of a baseline assessment.

Pulse Rate

Pulse rate is normally recorded as **beats per minute** (**bpm**).

The average pulse rate is 60–80bpm.

To take your pulse rate...

- press firmly with your index and middle finger on the artery in your wrist or arm
- count the number of beats for 60 seconds.

Blood Pressure

Blood pressure is the pressure of the blood against the walls of the **arteries**.

Two numbers are associated with blood pressure:

- The higher (**systolic**) number represents the pressure as the heart contracts (beats).
- The lower (**diastolic**) number represents the pressure when the heart relaxes.

The systolic pressure is stated first and the diastolic pressure second. An average blood pressure is 120/80mmHg.

Blood pressure can be measured using a **sphygmomanometer** or **electronic sensor**:

- A cuff is placed on the upper arm. It is inflated to stop blood flow.
- The pressure is released.

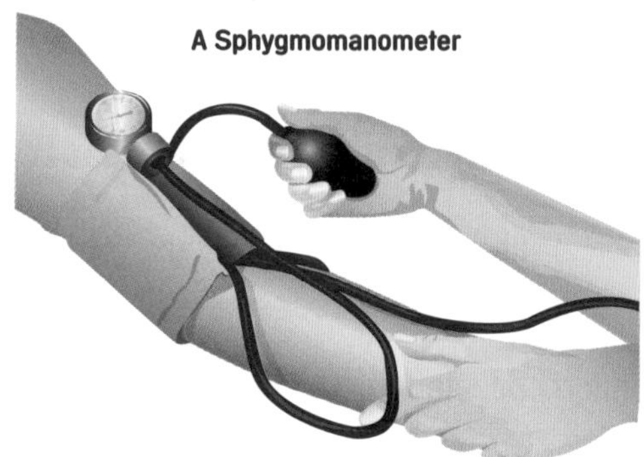

A Sphygmomanometer

- Sounds of the returning blood flow are listened for using a stethoscope under the cuff, and read off the display as the upper (when a pulse is heard) and lower (when the sound becomes continuous) numbers.

Electronic sensors, used on the upper arm or wrist, can now be used to measure blood pressure. The cuff can inflate automatically. A read-out is given on the machine, which also records heart rate.

Body Temperature

Body temperature is measured in degrees **Celsius** (**°C**). The average body temperature is 37°C.

A reading can be taken by placing...

- a sterile clinical thermometer in your mouth. The thermometer is shaken to return the mercury in the thermometer to the bulb. It is then placed under the tongue, left for three minutes, and read
- an electronic sensor thermometer in your ear. The temperature is read from the digital display
- a liquid crystal thermometer on your forehead. This gives a temperature read-out.

Clinical thermometers and electronic sensors have high accuracy and precision. Forehead thermometers do not, but are useful for indicating a fever.

Key Words Pulse rate • Blood pressure • Artery

Responding to Temperature Change

The average body temperature in humans is 37°C. If your temperature differs from this you will feel unwell and your body's systems may fail.

HT Your skin contains **receptors** that detect changes in temperature.

In **hot** conditions…
- blood vessels in your skin (**capillaries**) dilate to increase heat loss
- skin gets redder
- water **evaporates** through pores as sweat to cool you down.

In **cold** conditions…
- skin capillaries constrict to reduce heat loss
- skin appears paler than normal.

If your body gets too cold you start **shivering**. Shivers are **involuntary muscle spasms** that warm up the muscles.

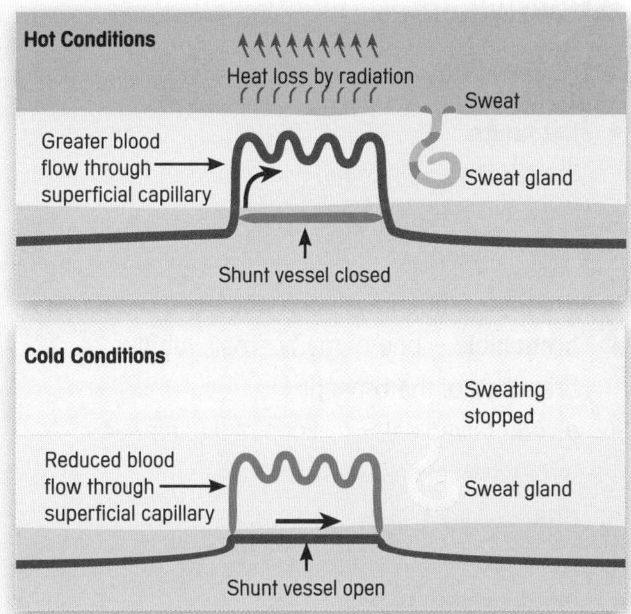

The Kidneys

Most people have two **kidneys**. Kidneys filter blood to…
- remove waste (urea)
- control the balance of water and other chemicals.

They achieve this by…
- filtering molecules from your blood to form **urine** (water, salt and urea)
- absorbing the sugar for **respiration**
- absorbing as much salt as your body needs
- sending the remaining urine to be stored in your bladder.

Your brain monitors water content, telling your kidneys to adjust the **concentration** and **volume** of urine they produce.

Low Water Level

When there's not enough water in the blood the kidneys produce small quantities of concentrated urine

High Water Level

When there's too much water in the blood the kidneys produce large quantities of dilute urine

Quick Test

1. What is the formula used to calculate BMI?
2. Give **two** functions of the kidneys.
3. HT What happens to the capillaries in the skin when a person gets hot?

Key Words

Receptor • Kidney

A1 Sport and Fitness

Understanding the Body

It's essential that sports and fitness practitioners understand how the human body works.

The Human Breathing System

The human breathing system contains...

- the **lungs**
- the **trachea** (windpipe) – the tube that delivers air to and from the lungs; it is surrounded by cartilage to prevent it collapsing
- **bronchi** (bronchus) – branches of the trachea
- **bronchiole** – one of many small, tubular branches of the bronchi
- **alveoli** (alveolus) – millions of tiny air sacs where gas exchange occurs
- **ribs** – protect the contents of the thorax (the region of the chest including the heart and lungs)
- **intercostal muscles** – found between the ribs; to raise and lower the ribs
- the **diaphragm** – a muscular 'sheet' dividing the thorax and abdomen.

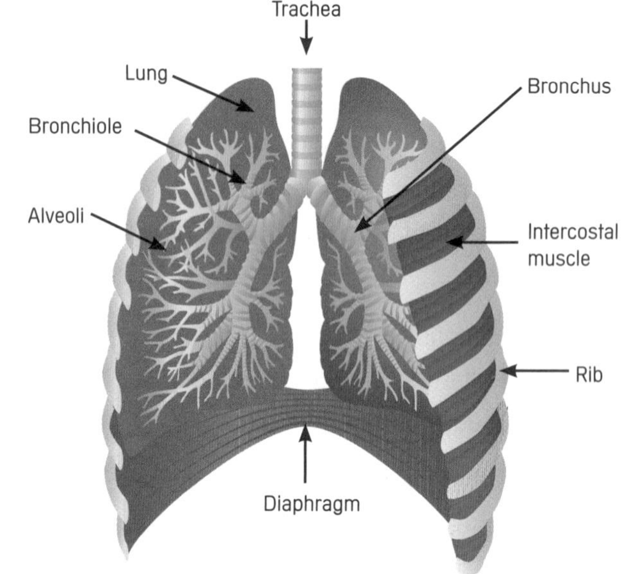

Ventilation

To efficiently exchange carbon dioxide and oxygen, the air in your lungs must be constantly refreshed.

To **inhale**, the volume of the thorax is increased:

- The **diaphragm contracts** to become flatter.
- The **intercostal muscles contract**, moving the ribcage upwards and outwards.

To **exhale**, the volume of the thorax is decreased:

- The **diaphragm relaxes**, returning back to its original position.
- The **intercostal muscles relax**, moving the ribcage downwards and inwards.

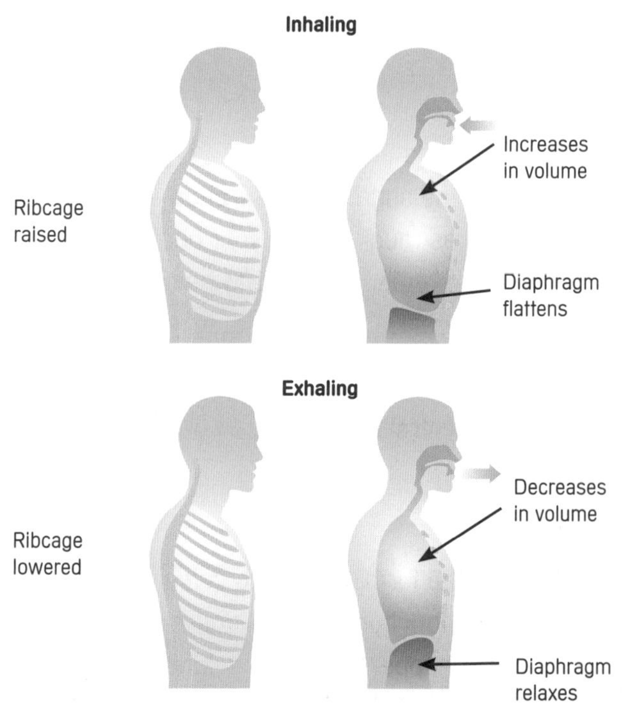

Key Words Lung • Trachea • Bronchus • Bronchiole • Alveolus • Rib • Intercostal muscles • Diaphragm

Blood

Red blood cells transport oxygen from the lungs to the body's cells. They have **no nucleus** and contain a red pigment called **haemoglobin**.

Plasma makes up about 55% of the blood volume. It **transports useful chemicals** such as glucose (used with oxygen for respiration) and **waste products** (including carbon dioxide and lactic acid, waste products of respiration in cells).

The other cells in the blood are **white blood cells**. These do have a nucleus. Their job is to **defend** the body against microorganisms.

Platelets are **cell fragments** found in blood plasma. When a blood vessel is damaged, platelets cause the blood to **clot**, stopping blood from leaving the body.

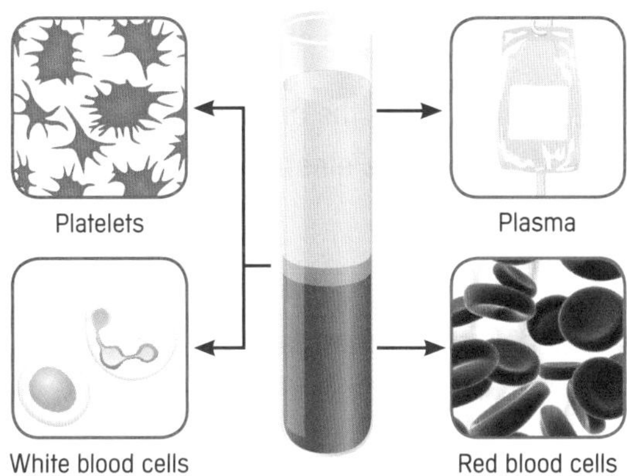

The Heart

Your **heart** is an organ in the circulatory system that pumps blood around your body. Most of the heart wall is made of muscle. It has four chambers:

- **Atria** (atrium) are the two smaller, less muscular upper chambers, which receive blood coming back to the heart.
- **Ventricles** are the two larger, more muscular lower chambers, which pump blood out of the heart.

This is how the heart pumps blood:

1. The **heart muscle relaxes**, allowing blood from the body into the atria.
2. The **atria contract**, squeezing blood into the ventricles.
3. The **ventricles contract**. Blood is carried to the lungs by the pulmonary arteries, and to the rest of the body by the aorta.
4. The **heart muscle relaxes**; the process starts again.

Valves ensure that the blood flows in the right direction.

Electrocardiograms (ECGs) can be used to study the functioning of the heart.

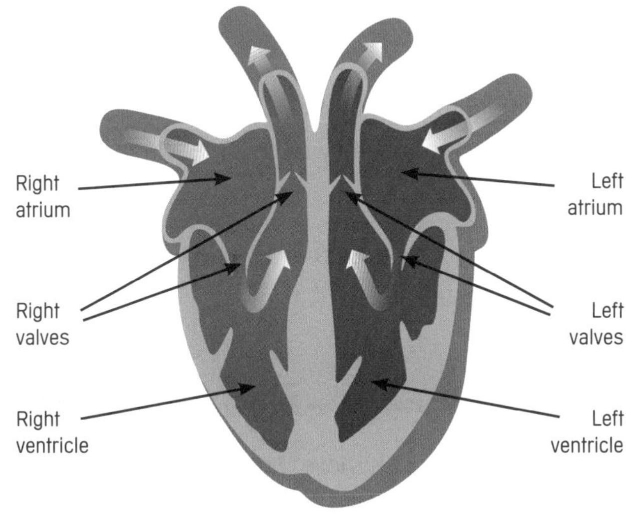

The left side of the heart is more muscular than the right because it has to pump blood around the whole body.

Quick Test

1. Which muscles cause the movement of the ribs?
2. **(a)** What is the function of red blood cells?
   (b) List the other components of the blood.
3. Which chambers of the heart deliver blood to the body?

Key Words Red blood cell • White blood cell • Platelet • Heart • Atrium • Ventricle • Valve

A1 Sport and Fitness

Blood Vessels

There are three types of blood vessel:

Arteries carry blood **away from the heart** towards the organs. Arteries have **thick, elastic walls** to cope with the high pressure of blood coming from the heart.

Veins carry blood from the organs **back to the heart**. They have **thinner, less elastic walls** and they contain **valves**.

Capillaries connect arteries to veins. They have **thin walls** to enable the **exchange of substances** between cells and the blood.

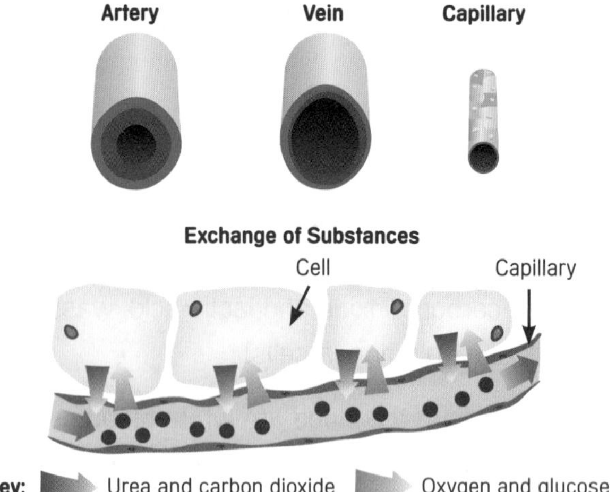

The Human Skeleton

Your skeleton has a number of functions:

- It **supports** your body.
- Parts of it enclose, and therefore **protect,** your organs.
- The attachment of **muscles** to various bones **allows you to move** by enabling parts to act as levers.

The bones of your skeleton are made of rigid connective tissue.

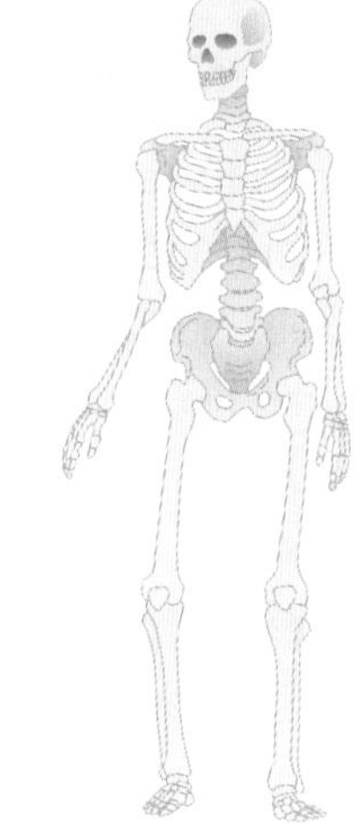

Joints

So that your body can move, bones are connected to each other at **joints**. The combination of bone, **cartilage**, muscle, **tendons** and **ligaments** enables your joints to move easily.

Muscle is tissue that can contract or be relaxed.

Ligaments are tough connective tissues that connect bones together in a joint. They are elastic enough to allow the bones to move.

Tendons connect muscles to bones. They are made from tough connective tissue that is inelastic.

Cartilage reduces friction between moving bones and acts as a shock absorber.

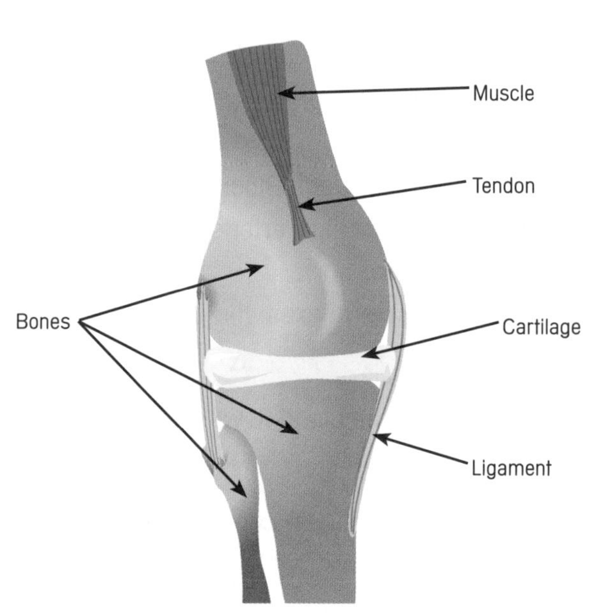

Key Words Artery • Vein • Capillary • Muscle • Cartilage • Tendon • Ligament

HT The Principle of Moments

During any kind of movement of the skeleton our bones act as **levers**.

The turning effect of a force on a lever is called a **moment**. The moment depends on the size of the force and its distance from the fulcrum:

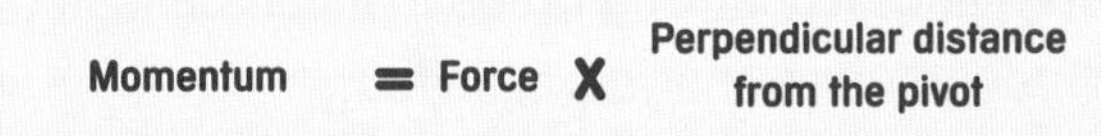

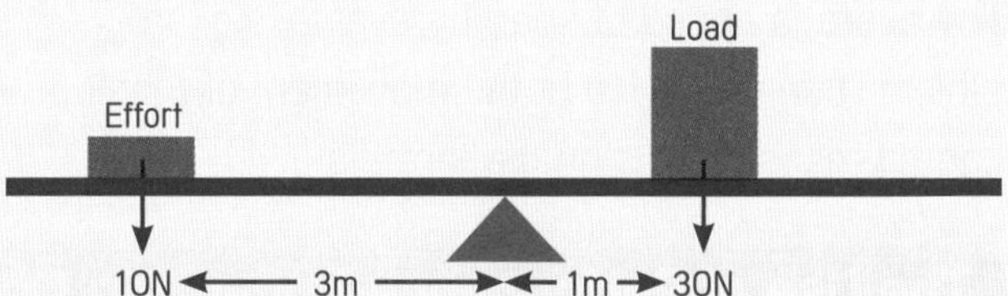

In the diagram, the moments on both sides of the fulcrum are equal (30Nm).
Note that a small force a long distance from the fulcrum can move a significant load.

Bones and Joints

In the lifting of an object...

- the elbow joint is the pivot or **fulcrum** (F)
- the biceps muscle provides the **effort** (E) to lift the load
- the object lifted is the **load** (L).

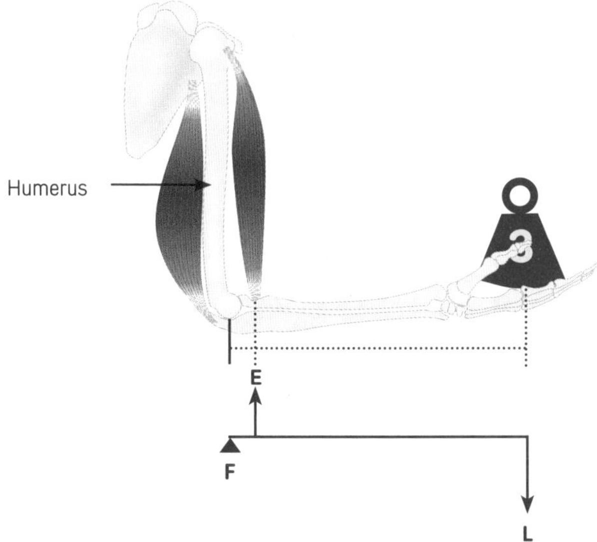

HT Using measurements of the distance of effort and load from the fulcrum and the force produced by the load, sports scientists can calculate and interpret information about forces needed by muscles for various activities.

For example, the biceps muscle is attached close to the elbow. The fulcrum is between the effort and the load.

So, the muscle must produce a large effort to lift a load, but a small movement of the muscle produces a large movement at the hand end.

Most lever systems in the human body produce large, fast movements rather than small powerful ones.

Quick Test

1. Give **one** feature of arteries that enables them to function.
2. Give **one** feature of veins that enables them to function.
3. Give **two** functions of the skeleton.
4. What is the name of the structure that connects a bone to a bone?
5. What is the name of the structure that connects a muscle to a bone?
6. HT Is this statement **true** or **false**? In a joint, the muscle is inserted between the fulcrum and the load. The muscle needs a small force to move the load.

Key Words Moment

A1 Sport and Fitness

Measuring Performance

The average speed of sporting events, e.g. an athlete running a race or the movement of a ball, can be measured using the formula:

$$\text{Average speed} = \frac{\text{Distance}}{\text{Time}}$$

The Use of Performance-Enhancing Drugs in Sport

Some athletes and sports people try to use banned drugs to improve their performance.

Many drugs, but not all, can be detected by testing the athlete's urine.

Performance-enhancing drugs that can be tested for through urine analysis include...

- anabolic steroids
- human growth hormone
- stimulants
- erythropoietin to improve oxygen-carrying capacity.

HT Improving Performance

Some scientists investigate **biomechanics**.

They study the sports person's movement and positioning. They use this information to improve performance.

Examples include...

- a golfer analysing their swing of the golf club
- a cricketer analysing how they play a shot, or bowl a ball
- a footballer analysing how their kicking of a ball affects its flight.

Training Programmes

Muscle-building exercises use weight-lifting programmes, with the appropriate nutrition, to build muscle mass.

Aerobic fitness exercises use a programme of regular vigorous exercise sessions increasing the heart rate and resulting in maximal oxygen consumption.

Physiotherapy

A **physiotherapist** specialises in the treatment of **skeletal-muscular injuries**.

Physiotherapists first assess the injury and then devise a set of **exercises** to aid recovery. The exercises are usually designed to **strengthen muscles**. For example, an injured leg could be treated with the following regime:

1. Warming up the joint by riding a stationary exercise bicycle.
2. Extending the leg while sitting.
3. Raising the leg while lying on the stomach.
4. Exercising in a pool.

Monitoring and Recording Progress

A treatment or fitness programme needs to be **monitored** to check that it's having the desired effect.

A programme can be **modified** before completion if the client is finding the programme...

- too **hard** (a new injury could occur)
- too **easy** (recovery would be slow).

Progress can be monitored during training by measuring your **pulse rate** or **aerobic fitness**.

Accurate, up-to-date records must be kept during treatment to **assess progress** and determine **trends**.

Progress records must take into account the **accuracy** and **reliability** of the recording techniques.

Personal Qualities of Practitioners

Health and fitness practitioners need to...

- have a professional yet caring manner
- encourage confidence and trust
- communicate effectively
- be able to work as a team
- make judgements if a client's statements conflict with other evidence
- develop a detached yet personal relationship with the client
- consider the patient, family, workplace and community as a whole.

Communication Skills

Physiotherapists must have good **communication skills** so they can...

- ask the client questions
- listen carefully to the client
- explain the treatment
- seek clarification about what the client says.

Quick Test

1. A cricket ball travels 60m to the boundary in 1.5 seconds. What is its speed?
2. Give **two** examples of performance-enhancing drugs.
3. What does a physiotherapist specialise in?
4. Give **two** reasons for keeping records during training programmes.

Key Words

Physiotherapist • Pulse rate

A1 Exam Practice Questions

1 Draw straight lines to join the words to the examples of lifestyle, health or fitness. **[2]**

Lifestyle	Claire goes swimming every day.
Health	Claire smokes 10 cigarettes a day.
Fitness	Claire is recovering from flu.

2 Which are steps involved in taking a pulse reading? Put ticks (✓) in the boxes next to the **two** correct options. **[2]**

Press softly with your thumb on the artery in your wrist or arm. ☐

Count the number of beats for 60 seconds. ☐

Count the number of alternate beats for 25 seconds. ☐

Press firmly with your index and middle finger on the artery in your wrist or arm. ☐

3 Which piece of equipment is used by a nurse to measure a person's…

(a) temperature? .... **[1]**

(b) blood pressure? .... **[1]**

4 Astra is 1.78m tall and has a mass of 90kg. The formula to calculate BMI is:

$$\text{BMI} = \frac{\text{Body mass in kg}}{[\text{Height in m}]^2}$$

(a) Calculate Astra's BMI. Show your working. **[2]**

....

(b) Use the information on page 5 to comment on Astra's BMI. **[1]**

....

5 Label the parts of the heart. **[3]**

A ....

B ....

C ....

6 (a) Complete the labels to identify the different components of blood. [4]

A ....

B ....

C ....

D ....

(b) Give the function of each component. [4]

A ....

B ....

C ....

D ....

7 An Olympic swimmer set a world record by completing an 800m race in 8 minutes 14 seconds. What was her average speed during the race? [2]

....

8 Complete the following statements about parts of the human breathing system. [4]

The .... is the tube that delivers air the lungs.

The .... is a sheet of skin and muscle that is lowered during breathing.

The .... move upwards and outwards as we breathe in.

The exchange of gases occurs across tiny structures called ....

9 Describe what happens in the human breathing system when a person breathes in.
The quality of written communication will be assessed in your answer to this question. [6]

....

....

....

....

....

....

HT 10 Explain why any risk to a client of a fitness programme must be assessed before the programme is started. [2]

....

....

A2 Health Care

Health Organisations

Health organisations work together to provide effective **life care**. Their work is regulated to make sure that high standards are maintained.

They operate locally, nationally or internationally.

Examples of local organisations include...
- health centres
- hospitals
- dentists
- opticians.

Local health centres provide you with medical treatment and advice. This may be...
- free – covered by the **National Health Service (NHS)**
- chargeable – classed as **private health care**.

Some of the services available include...
- medical examinations
- counselling
- family planning (contraception).

The National Health Service

The National Health Service...
- makes health care available to all citizens
- can provide specialist care if it's not available locally.

The management of the National Health Service needs to...
- monitor national trends in public health (e.g. flu outbreaks)
- plan suitable health care
- allocate resources (e.g. staff and equipment) where and when they are needed.

Emergency Treatment

Like all parts of the National Health Service, the Accident and Emergency (A&E) department of a hospital has to manage its resources to make sure that they are used most effectively.

For example, money should be spent on suitable equipment. A rural hospital is unlikely to need equipment to treat multiple victims of motorway accidents.

Paramedics and nurses in A&E departments in hospitals operate a policy of **triage**. This is a method of prioritising patients based on how life-threatening their injuries are. For example, a person who has stopped breathing would be treated before a patient with a broken leg.

A&E departments train and practise for if a major incident occurs. This helps to assess...
- what would be required should one of these incidents occur
- whether sufficient staff and equipment would be available.

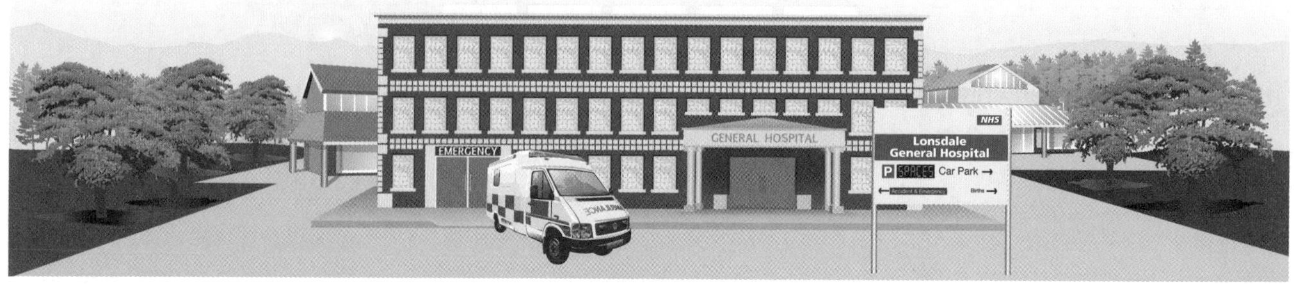

Health Care Practitioners

Practitioners have special training to help you maintain and improve your health.

Examples of practitioners include...

- doctors
- dentists
- registered nurses
- opticians.

A **registered nurse** plans health care and provides advice if you have an acute illness. Their duties include...

- administering medication, treatments and injections with instructions from the doctor
- taking blood tests
- observing patients for changes
- checking vital signs
- maintaining health records.

An **optician** carries out detailed eye examinations to test a client's vision. This will identify...

- problems with vision and eye defects
- eye injuries
- problems with ill-health, such as diabetes and high blood pressure.

Opticians use a range of instruments and charts to assess a person's vision. They prescribe lenses, either spectacles or contact lenses, to correct defects in vision.

Regular contact with the patient and practitioner means that the practitioner gets to know the patient's medical history and the contact increases **trust**.

Health and safety **regulations** affect the work that medical practitioners do. For example, in treatments and medicines that they provide, facilities in surgeries, and issues to consider when visiting patients.

Discussing Health Issues

Health issues are brought to the public's attention through **education** and **public information programmes**. Programmes include...

- the benefits of vaccination
- how lifestyle can improve health
- treatments that are available
- the success rates of operations
- survival time after treatment.

Raising public awareness is important because it can reduce illness or disease and enable people to make decisions about treatment that is available or offered to them.

Health education is expensive but can be **cost effective** in the long term as it can save money that would otherwise be spent on treatments.

Lifestyle and Medical History

Practitioners will ask about your medical history or lifestyle before any treatment can begin.

HT This is to ensure that the suggested treatment is effective and will not cause you any damaging effects.

A practitioner needs to be made aware of the following factors:

Symptoms – these can be used to identify a health problem.

Current medication – different medicines can sometimes conflict with one another.

Alcohol consumption – excessive alcohol intake can cause...

- weight gain
- damage to the liver and kidneys
- interference with some medications.

Tobacco use – smoking has been directly linked with...

- lung cancer
- heart disease
- high blood pressure.

Level of physical activity – lack of exercise can lead to...

- depression
- obesity
- problems with sleeping and concentration.

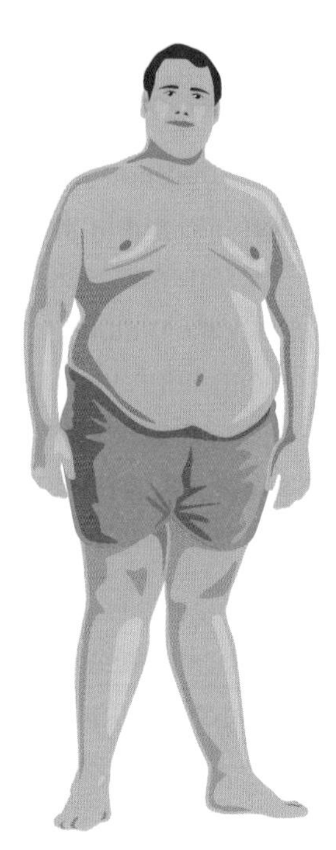

Family medical history – some medical conditions can be **genetic** (inherited). It's important to know if any particular conditions run in your family.

Previous treatments – recurring symptoms might require you to have a different **diagnosis** or to see a specialist.

Allergies – it is important for the practitioner to know about the patient's allergies. These may affect the medicines that are prescribed or the treatments given.

Key Words Practitioner • Symptom • Genetic • Diagnosis

Reasons for Assessment

You must be properly assessed before any diagnostic tests are carried out to ensure that the tests will not make your condition worse.

The risk of carrying out any test or procedure will be balanced against the advantages of making a diagnosis or being able to treat the symptoms.

Medical Treatments

After a consultation with your doctor (GP), you may be referred to a consultant for specialist treatment.

All **treatments** carry **risks** that have to be weighed up against their potential **benefits**.
A treatment might...

- cause further harm
- cause **side effects**
- allow the review of different practices used in treatment.

Before you undertake a medical treatment your informed **consent** (agreement) needs to be obtained.

HT Recording Information

Your health information must be recorded, stored and made available to other people on the practitioner's team.

Health records are useful because...

- your medical history may help the doctor in his or her diagnosis of your current health problem
- they tell the doctor about any allergies to medicines you have or serious medical conditions
- another practitioner can treat you if your regular practitioner is unavailable
- they include full records of treatments you have had previously, including in different parts of the NHS, e.g. not only from your GP but also from A&E, specialists and hospital treatment
- the diagnosis or procedures can be investigated if something goes wrong
- they allow the review of different practices used in treatment.

Quick Test

1. What is the method used to prioritise the treatment of patients in A&E departments?
2. Give **two** things a practitioner will ask about the medical history of a patient.
3. Write down **two** possible effects of lack of exercise.
4. HT Give **two** reasons why information about a patient's health is recorded.

Key Words Side effect

A2 Health Care

The Female Reproductive System

The **female reproductive system** is designed to carry and give birth to babies.

Eggs develop in the **ovaries**. A single egg is released each month.

The released egg travels along the **fallopian tubes** where it may be fertilised. **Fertilisation** occurs after sexual intercourse when a sperm fuses with an egg.

A fertilised egg reaches the **uterus** where it implants into the thickened lining and **develops into a baby**.

The **cervix** is a ring of **muscle** that allows sperm to enter during sexual intercourse or menstrual blood to leave during a period.

The **vagina** is the tube leading to the cervix. It **widens** during sexual intercourse and childbirth.

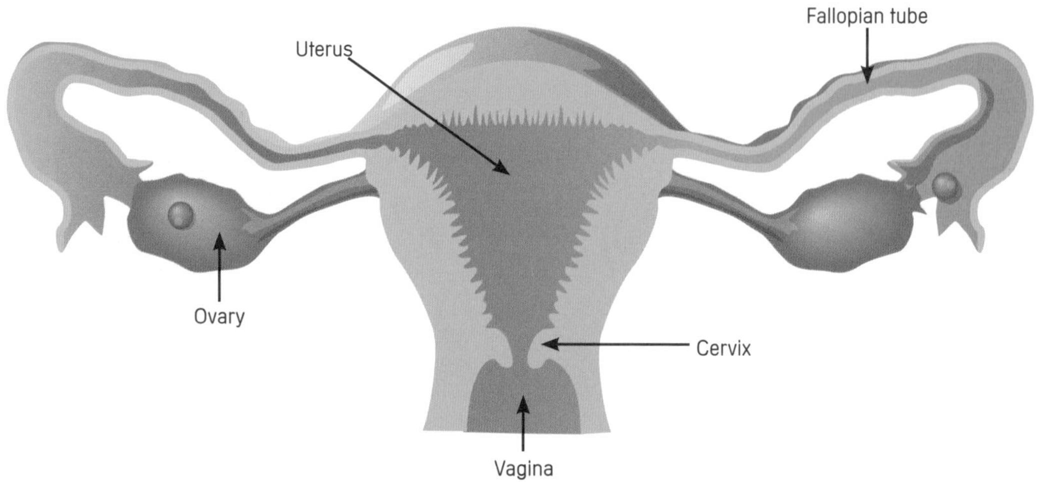

The Menstrual Cycle

A woman is **fertile** between the ages of approximately 13 and 50.

Every month, a woman's body goes through a cycle called the **menstrual cycle**. During this cycle, an egg is released from her ovaries. The uterus also thickens to receive the egg, if it becomes fertilised. This thickened lining of the uterus is broken down if an egg is not fertilised.

These are the stages of the menstrual cycle:

1. The uterus lining breaks down and the woman has a period.
2. The uterus wall is repaired. **Oestrogen** causes the uterus lining to thicken.
3. An egg is released by the ovary.
4. **Progesterone** makes the lining stay thick waiting for a fertilised egg.
5. If no fertilised egg is detected the cycle restarts.

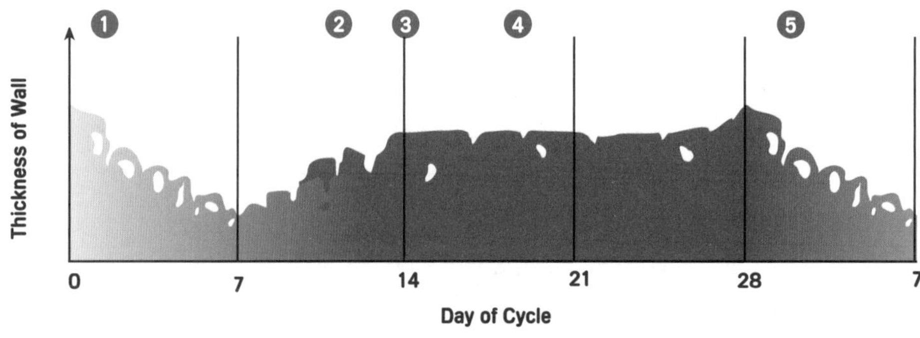

Key Words Fertilisation • Menstrual cycle • Oestrogen • Progesterone

In-Vitro Fertilisation

***In-vitro* fertilisation** (**IVF**) is used to help a couple have a baby when one or both partners have a fertility problem.

The process begins with counselling. This…

- explores the fertility problem
- prepares the couple for the success or failure of the treatment
- provides emotional support.

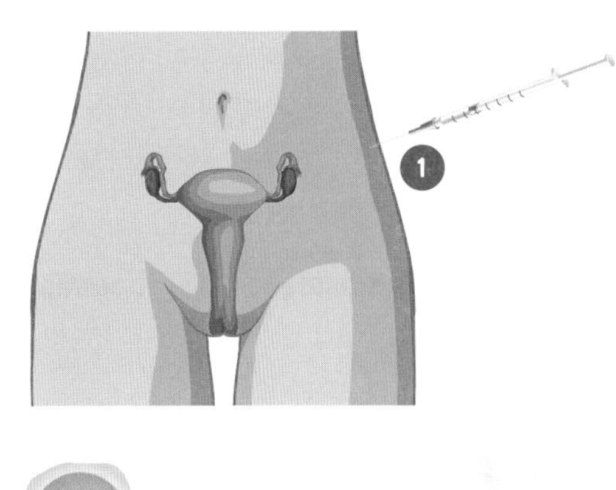

These are the stages of IVF:

1. The woman is given hormone treatment. (Follicle stimulating hormone (FSH) to stimulate egg production and human chorionic gonadotrophin (HCG) to cause the follicles to mature.)
2. Eggs are collected from the ovaries.
3. A sperm sample is provided by the father.
4. The eggs are mixed with the sperm and checked for fertilisation.
5. The **embryo** is allowed to develop for five days.
6. The embryo is implanted in the mother.

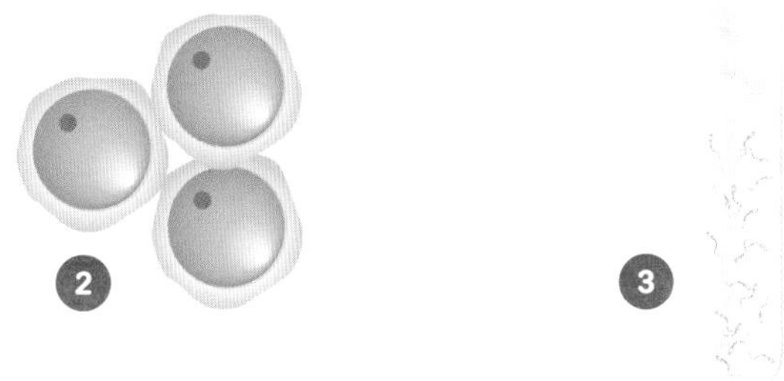

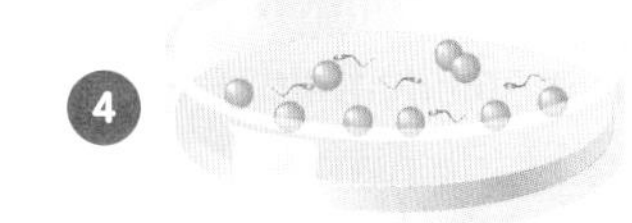

After IVF, **monitoring** takes place:

- A pregnancy test after two weeks – if IVF was successful, the embryo will implant in the uterus wall.
- An **ultrasound scan** after six weeks – essential to check the growth of the embryo.

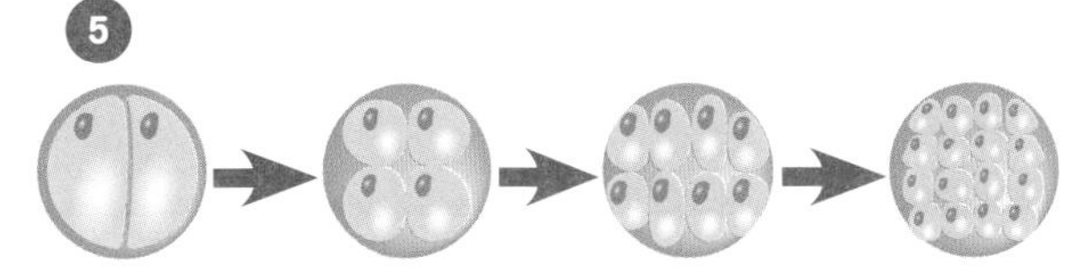

Because more than one embryo may be transferred to the uterus, there has been a greater than usual chance of **multiple births**. The mother may have twins or triplets.

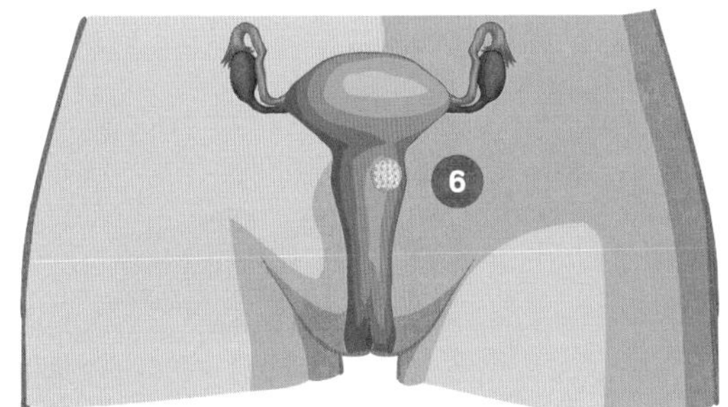

Quick Test

1. Where are eggs fertilised?
2. What is the function of oestrogen?
3. In what part of the reproductive system does the embryo develop during pregnancy?
4. Give **two** functions of counselling before a programme of IVF.
5. Following IVF, when is the embryo transferred to the mother?
6. Give **two** ways in which successful implantation and development of the embryo are monitored.

Key Words ***In-vitro* fertilisation • Embryo • Monitoring • Ultrasound scan**

Pregnancy

During **pregnancy** the ovaries stop developing eggs. The embryo moves to the uterus, where it develops. After around two months, the embryo becomes a foetus.

Several changes occur in the reproductive system:

- A **placenta**, **umbilical cord** and **amnion** (amniotic sac) are produced.
- The **foetus grows** in length.
- The **uterus expands**.

The placenta is made of soft, spongy tissue. It...

- delivers food and oxygen to the foetus
- removes waste from the foetus.

The **umbilical cord** contains blood vessels. These carry blood between the foetus and the placenta.

The baby develops in the **amnion** (**amniotic sac**) which is filled with **amniotic fluid**. The amniotic sac...

- keeps the baby at the right temperature
- protects the baby from getting bumped.

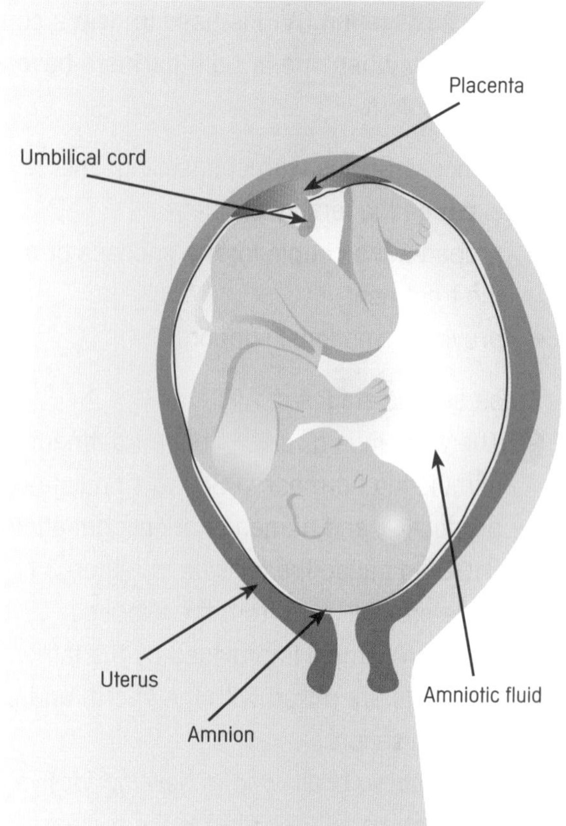

Birth

There are four stages of **labour** (childbirth):

1. The uterus contracts so the baby's head lines up with the cervix.

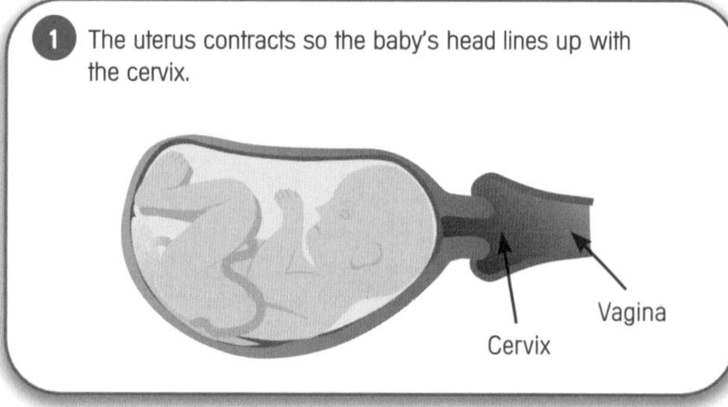

2. The cervix widens and the mucus plug pops out. This allows the amniotic fluid to flow out through the vagina (known as 'waters breaking').

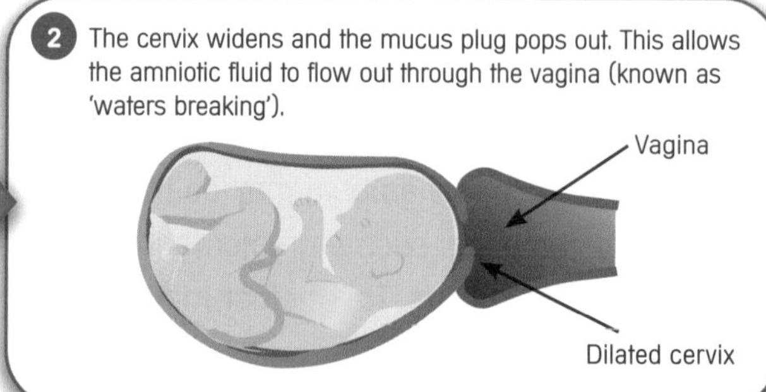

3. **Contractions** become stronger and more frequent. The mother has a strong urge to push and the baby is born.

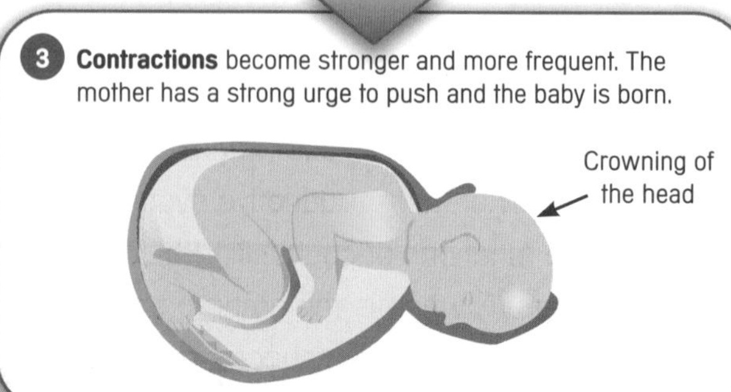

4. The umbilical cord and placenta come away from the uterus wall. Further contractions cause them (known as the 'afterbirth') to pass out of the vagina.

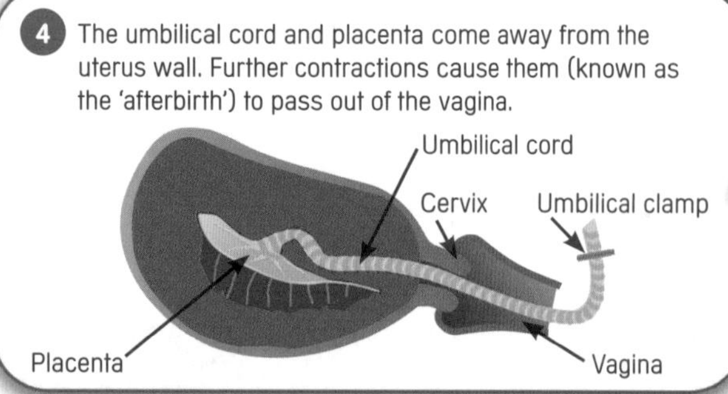

Key Words Placenta • Umbilical cord • Amnion • Amniotic fluid

Antenatal Care

Antenatal care is care provided during pregnancy.

The midwife...
- plans care during pregnancy
- provides information on nutrition, food hygiene, medicines and lifestyle
- organises screening programme and place of birth
- prepares for labour and birth.

Monitoring involves ultrasound scans and recording weight and blood pressure.

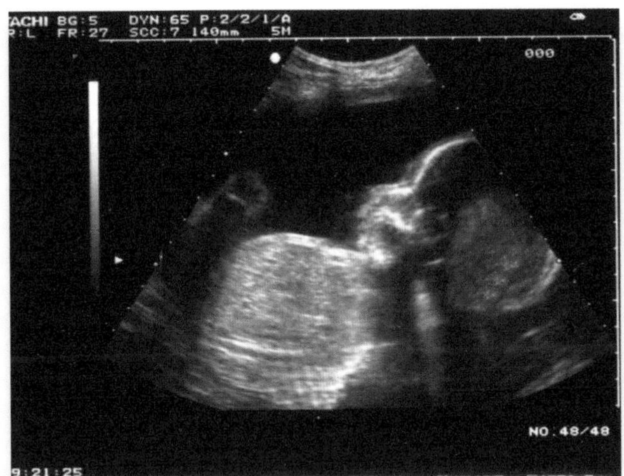

Conditions that can Affect Health During Pregnancy

Some conditions that occur during pregnancy can be hazardous to the mother and/or child.

Condition	Cause	Diagnosis
Gestational diabetes	Lack of the hormone insulin in the mother's blood	**Glucose tolerance test** • After a glucose drink is given to the mother, the time taken for the removal of glucose from the blood is measured. **Urine test** • The mother's urine is tested for the presence of glucose.
Pre-eclampsia	Thought to occur if the placenta isn't working properly	**Blood pressure measurement** • Mother's blood pressure is high. **Urine test** • Protein is present in the mother's urine.

Quick Test

1. What is contained within the amnion?
2. Give **two** functions of the placenta.
3. What does the umbilical cord contain?
4. What is the cause of gestational diabetes?

Key Words

Antenatal care

A2 Health Care

Blood Testing

Blood testing can detect several problems with the foetus and mother during pregnancy.

Anaemia is a condition that occurs if a person is deficient in iron. The person will not produce enough red blood cells.

Women – and the foetus – can become anaemic during pregnancy because of the increased demand for iron and vitamins as the foetus grows.

To detect anaemia, blood tests are carried out at the beginning of pregnancy and in the second half of pregnancy.

Down's syndrome is a genetic defect. Several tests are available to test for a foetus with Down's syndrome.

Two types of blood test can be carried out at different times during pregnancy. High levels of particular **hormones** and **proteins** in the mother's blood can give an accurate diagnosis of Down's syndrome.

Spina bifida is a birth defect that occurs if one or more of the vertebrae in the spine do not form properly. It has environmental and genetic causes. Blood tests and scans during pregnancy detect about 90% of cases.

Taking a Blood Sample

A blood sample can be taken in the following way:

1. A pressure collar is applied to the upper arm
2. The skin is wiped with an **antiseptic** to sterilise it.
3. A vein is selected.
4. The needle of a sterile **syringe** is inserted into the vein.
5. The **vacuum** inside the syringe draws blood in.
6. The blood sample is placed into a sample tube. A **preservative** keeps the blood under the right conditions for testing.
7. The health practitioner ensures that the sample is correctly labelled.

The blood sample can then be tested for chemicals or observed under a microscope.

Taking a Blood Sample

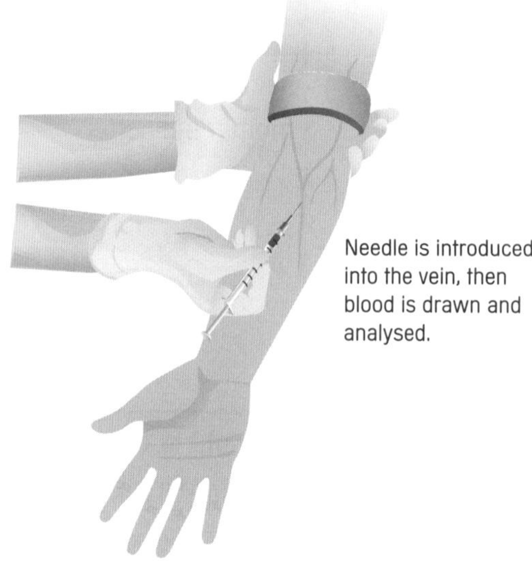

Needle is introduced into the vein, then blood is drawn and analysed.

Testing a Urine Sample

Test sticks containing chemicals or **enzymes** can be used to analyse urine samples.

The sticks change colour if they detect different substances.

There are different types of stick test for different chemicals, including glucose and protein.

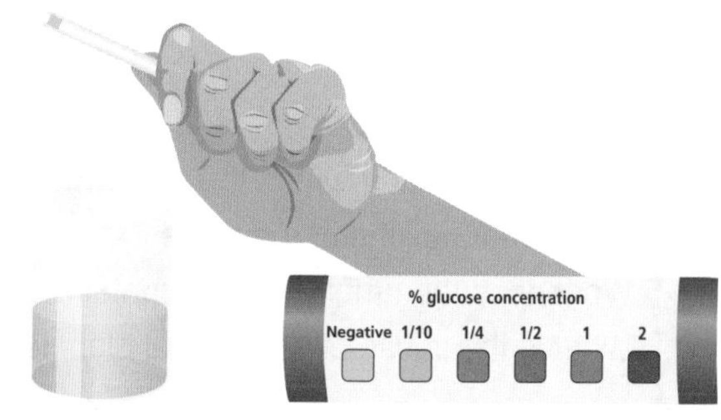

Key Words Enzyme

Post-Natal Care

Post-natal care is provided after the birth of the baby.

The health of the baby and mother is monitored at various stages of post-natal care.

The **APGAR score** assesses the health of the newborn baby 1 minute and 5 minutes after birth to see if the baby has any immediate problems that need medical support:

	Scores 0	Scores 1	Scores 2
Appearance	Blue or pale all over	Pink body but pale or blue fingers	Pink all over
Pulse	0bpm	Less than 100bpm	100bpm or more
Grimace	No response to stimulation	Feeble grimace or cry when stimulated	Cry or pull away when stimulated
Activity	No bending of joints	Some bending of joints	Bending of joints that resists straightening
Respiration	No breathing	Weak, irregular breathing	Strong, deep, regular breathing

An APGAR score of...

- less than 5 = low. May be a cause for concern. The APGAR test is used again after five minutes and again, if necessary. Medical treatment may be required
- 5–7 = fair condition. May require some help
- 8–10 = good to excellent condition.

Growth charts are used to monitor and compare the child's growth with UK and world data from healthy children.

Draw lines through the child's age and weight. Check the percentile where they cross. A 50th percentile, for instance, means that the child weighs more than about 50% of children of his or her age.

Growth Chart

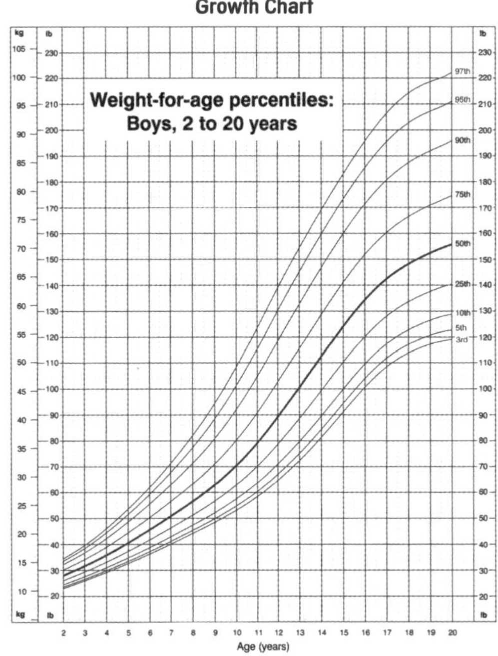

Development tests monitor the baby's weight, length, reflexes, motor skills, responses to light and sound and skin condition.

The baby and mother are visited for the first few days by the midwife. Care is then transferred back to the doctor and **health care visitor**. Later it is transferred to the doctor and **visits to the clinic**.

Quick Test

1. When taking a blood sample, give two ways in which infection of the patient is avoided.
2. Name a test carried out on a newborn baby.
3. List **three** assessments that are made in post-natal development tests.

Key Words

Post-natal care

A2 Exam Practice Questions

1 Give **two** functions of the National Health Service. [2]

2 Label the parts of the human female reproductive system. [3]

A

C

B

3 When and why are the following used?

(a) Ultrasound scan [1]

(b) Growth charts [1]

(c) Triage [1]

(d) Consent form [1]

4 **(a)** The following are the stages of *in-vitro* fertilisation (IVF).
Put a tick (✓) in the box next to the first stage of the treatment. [1]

Implantation	
Fertilisation	
Collection of eggs	
Hormone treatment	

(b) Why is the chance of multiple births increased by IVF? [1]

5 Draw straight lines to match the parts of the reproductive system during pregnancy with the correct statements. **[3]**

Part	Statement
Amniotic fluid	Where fertilisation occurs
Fallopian tube	Absorbs shock and stops the baby from getting bumped
Placenta	Expands to accommodate the foetus during development
Uterus	Delivers food and oxygen to the foetus

6 Complete the empty columns of the table to give **one** test for gestational diabetes and **one** test for pre-eclampsia. **[4]**

Name of Condition During Pregnancy	Test	Evidence Leading to Diagnosis
Gestational diabetes		
Pre-eclampsia		

7 What does the APGAR score assess and why? **[2]**

HT 8 Explain why personal medical information must be recorded, stored and made available to other medical practitioners.

The quality of written communication will be assessed in your answer to this question. **[6]**

A3 Monitoring and Protecting the Environment

Environmental Protection

Individual people, organisations and governments work to protect the environment.

The work involves ecologists, energy managers, environmental managers, environmental consultants, recycling officers and conservation officers.

The role of **environment protection officers** is very varied. Their activities can include...

- monitoring industrial sites
- checking for water pollution
- checking flood risks
- monitoring air quality
- protecting wildlife.

Practitioners working in environmental protection need the necessary scientific and technical skills to analyse and interpret the environment and the information they collect. They must follow health and safety regulations to avoid injury to themselves in the laboratory and the field or damage to the environment.

Accreditation

It's essential that any scientific data collected is **accurate** and **reliable**. Important decisions may be based on the evidence they produce.

The collection of accurate and reliable evidence can allow for a **valid** and **justifiable** conclusion so that the right decision is made.

Many public laboratories have a system of **accreditation**. Accreditation is used to check the accuracy and precision of a laboratory's results and give clients confidence.

Good laboratory practice depends on...

- adherence to health and safety regulations
- continual development of staff
- regular maintenance and checking of equipment and instruments.

Key Words Accreditation

Accurate Evidence

Proficiency tests are carried out to check the accuracy of analytical procedures:

1. Identical samples are sent to a group of laboratories.
2. Each laboratory analyses the sample.
3. The results are compiled.
4. A report is circulated to the laboratories.
5. The tests highlight laboratories whose results differ from the rest.

Taking Samples

It's important that samples are **representative** of the area that's being investigated. Samples taken from an area of a field that's shaded by trees, for example, may not be the same as samples from the centre.

A scientist collects representative samples by collecting multiple samples at random across the area.

If the sample is changed in any way then it's no longer **reliable**.

Using a system of **common practices** and **procedures** can increase reliability because...

- there is less room for human error
- tests can be repeated on the same sample.

Samples should be stored in a sterile container at a suitable temperature to prevent change or **deterioration**.

The container should be sealed, labelled and stored in a safe place to avoid...

- contamination
- tampering.

Quick Test

1. Why do labs undergo accreditation?
2. Give **three** factors that good laboratory practice depends on.
3. What is a proficiency test?
4. Give **two** reasons why samples are sealed after collection.

A3 Monitoring and Protecting the Environment

Monitoring the Effects of Climate Change in the Oceans

Scientists identify and monitor the **organisms** present in the oceans.

Climate change is increasing the temperature of the oceans.

As the oceans warm up…

- species of plankton, fish and invertebrates that live in colder water move northwards
- species that live in the most northerly regions may become extinct.

An example of this change in distribution can be seen in the John Dory fish.

This movement affects **food chains** and fish and bird **populations** in the colder and warmer areas.

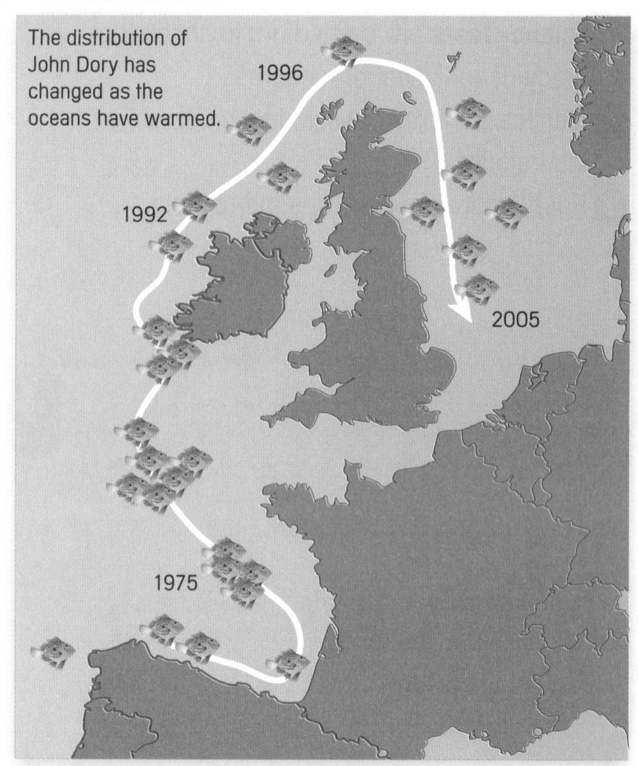

The distribution of John Dory has changed as the oceans have warmed.
1996
1992
2005
1975

Monitoring Pollution in Fresh Water

Scientists use **indicator organisms** or **indicator species** to measure the level of pollution in fresh water.

Certain fresh-water invertebrates (animals without backbones) can only live in very clean water; others can live in polluted water.

Environmental scientists sample and record the invertebrates in ponds, streams, rivers and canals.

The presence of certain animals in the water and the absence of others gives them a good idea of the level of pollution in the water.

This is called a **biotic index**.

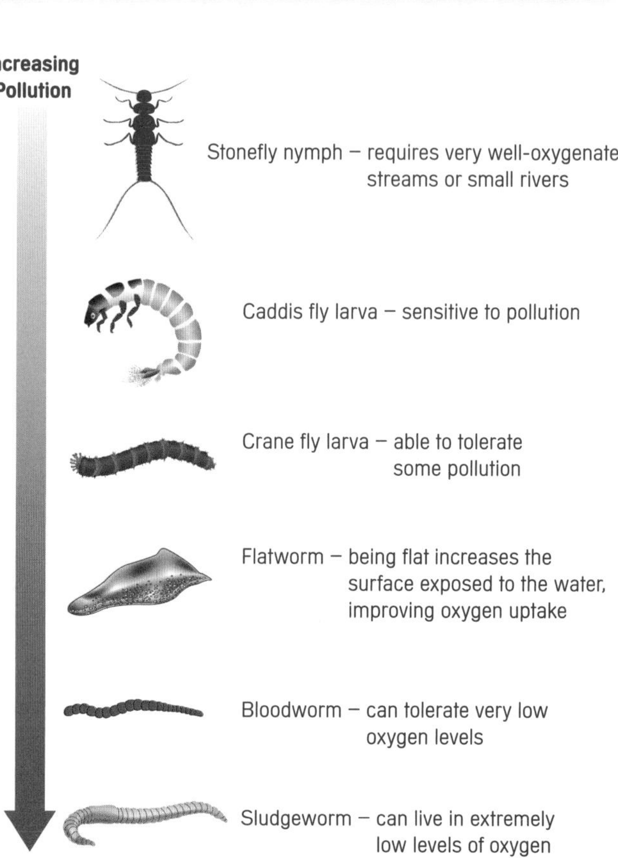

Increasing Pollution
Stonefly nymph – requires very well-oxygenated streams or small rivers
Caddis fly larva – sensitive to pollution
Crane fly larva – able to tolerate some pollution
Flatworm – being flat increases the surface exposed to the water, improving oxygen uptake
Bloodworm – can tolerate very low oxygen levels
Sludgeworm – can live in extremely low levels of oxygen

Key Words Organism • Indicator organism • Indicator species

Visual Examination

Visual examination of the environment gives quick results.

Images can be recorded in different ways, including written descriptions, drawings, photographs and videos.

The method chosen will depend on the level of detail required in order to be able to identify important features and the type of information required.

For example...

- written descriptions to give detail that can't be recorded in another way, such as the weather when a study was made
- a sketch or drawing to make a quick record, where accuracy is not required or to give detail that can't be recorded in a photograph
- a photograph would be taken to show accurate detail, such as the structure of an organism
- a video would be made to show movement of, for example, an organism.

Features of an Image

Sharpness of focus	**Contrast**	**Depth of field**	**Magnification**
Whether the image seen is sharp or blurred	The extent to which parts of the image stand out from other objects and the background	The extent to which an object or objects at different distances from the camera are in focus	The size of the image in relation to the size of the object.

The image is sharp.	**Contrast is normal.**	**Wide depth of field. The flower and leaves are in focus.**	**Original object. No magnification.**
	Contrast is low.		

The image is not sharp. It is out of focus.	**Contrast is too high.**	**Narrow depth of field. Only the centre of the flower is in focus.**	**x3 magnification. Image appears three times as large as the object.**

Quick Test

1. Give **three** ways of recording visual images.
2. What is the depth of field of an image?
3. How can the sampling of ocean organisms provide evidence for climate change?
4. What is an indicator organism?

Key Words Sharpness of focus • Contrast • Depth of field • Magnification

A3 Monitoring and Protecting the Environment

Taking Measurements

Measurements can be taken from an image or an object using a **linear scale**, such as a ruler.

If a measurement falls **between graduations** on the linear scale, it can be **estimated**. For example, this ruler shows a measurement of 6.05cm.

HT You need to ensure that graduations on the linear scale are clear. If not, inaccurate readings might be taken, leading to systematic errors.

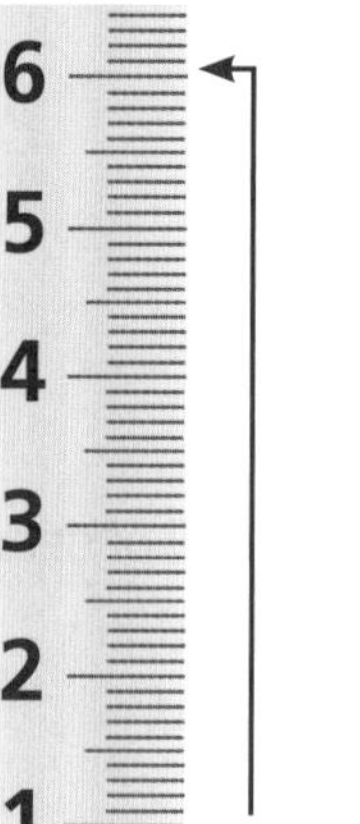

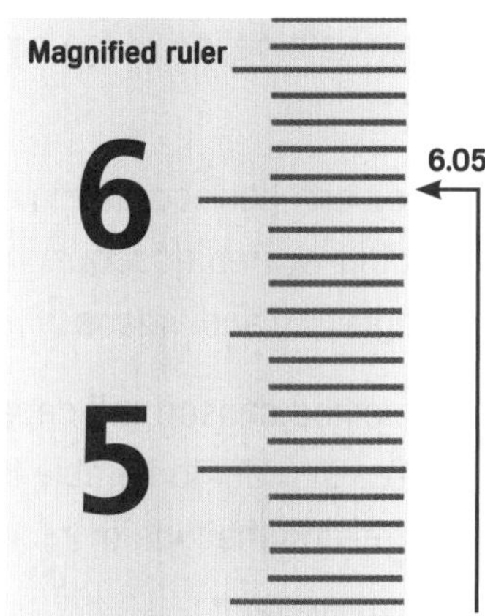

Error in Measurements

The **error** is the difference between the measured value and the **true value**.

Error is what causes values to be different when measurements are repeated.

HT Accuracy, Precision and Uncertainty

When taking measurements, the **accuracy** of the measurement is how close it is to the true value.

Precision is the closeness of agreement between a series of measurements.

Error leads to **uncertainty** in measurements.

Uncertainty can arise from...

- random error
- systematic error.

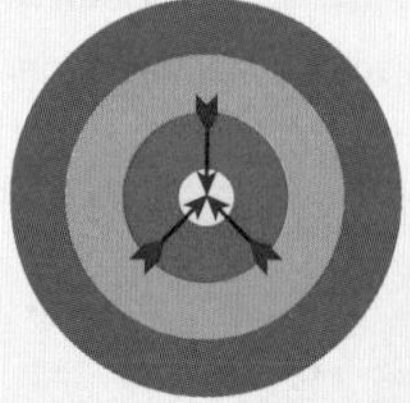

Accurate and precise

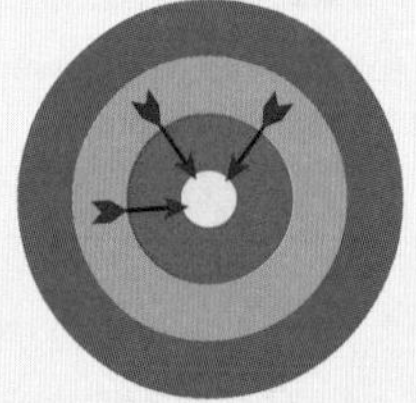

Accurate but imprecise

Precise but inaccurate

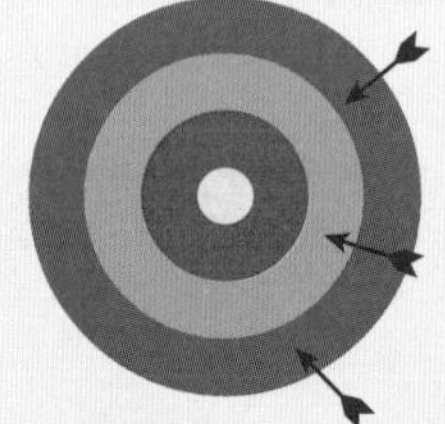

Inaccurate and imprecise

	Definition	Possible Causes
Random error	Over a number of measurements, values vary in an unpredictable way.	• Low sensitivity of equipment • It's difficult to make measurements, e.g. at the growing point of a plant
Systematic error	The values measured are different from the true value in a consistent way, either consistently higher or consistently lower.	• An incorrectly calibrated instrument • The operator taking measurements that are consistently incorrect

Key Words Error • Accuracy • Precision • Uncertainty

Monitoring and Protecting the Environment A3

HT Data Collection

The repeatability and reproducibility of data can be increased using a system of common practice.

The **repeatability** of data depends on the ability of a person or group of investigators to obtain similar results when carrying out the investigation several times.

The **reproducibility** of data depends on the variability of data when different scientists, for instance, in different laboratories, are carrying out the same investigation.

Calculating Measurements

Linear measurements can be used to calculate the area of various shapes. Here are some examples:

- **Squares**

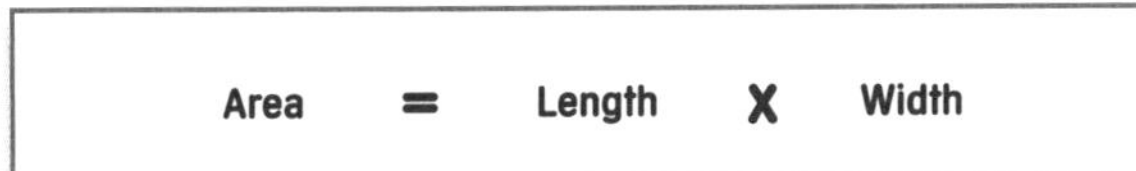

- **Rectangles**

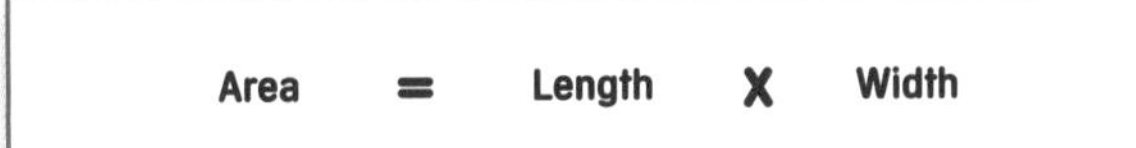

- **Irregular shapes**
  Divide the shape up into equal-sized squares. Measure the length of one square and calculate its area. Then multiply the area by the total number of squares.

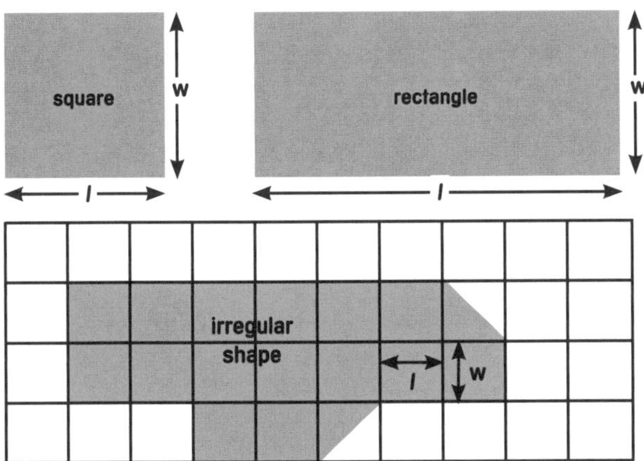

HT A calculated area has a greater level of **uncertainty** than a single measured length. This is because area is calculated from more than one length, each with a degree of uncertainty.

The area of an irregular object can be found by counting the squares on the graph paper.

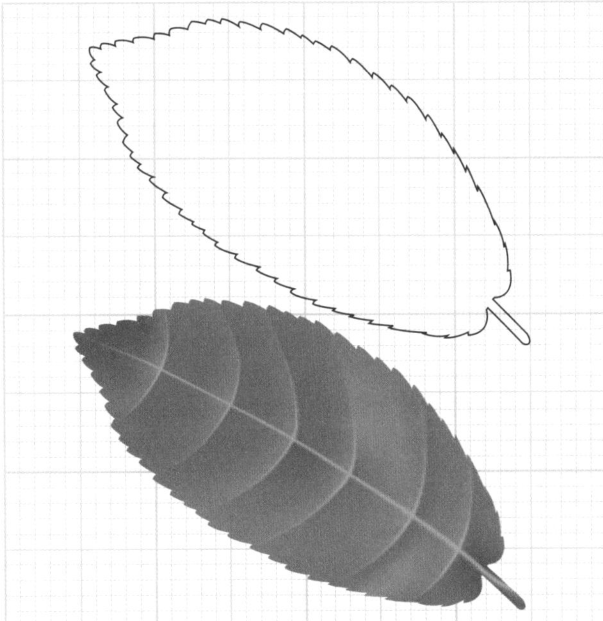

Quick Test

1. Calculate the area of a field 250m long and 120m wide.
2. HT Give two types of error that lead to uncertainty.
3. HT Five different thermometers each gave different readings in the science lab. What term is used to describe these measurements?
4. HT Why does the value of an area that has been calculated have a greater uncertainty than the value of its length or width?

A3 Monitoring and Protecting the Environment

Colour Matching

Colour matching is used in analysis to give both **qualitative** and **semi-quantitative** information.

Qualitative tests are identification tests. They detect the presence of substances. Quantitative tests tell you how much of a substance is present.

Litmus tests use colour to show whether a solution is **acid** or **alkali**. Litmus turns **red** in acid and **blue** in alkali. This is an example of a **qualitative** test.

Semi-quantitative tests give an approximate quantity or value of a substance in a sample, i.e. they are more precise than qualitative tests.

An example of a semi-quantitative test that relies on colour is the use of **universal indicator** to determine the pH of a solution.

The **pH scale** is a measure of acidity or alkalinity. It's more accurate than litmus but still requires a visual reading.

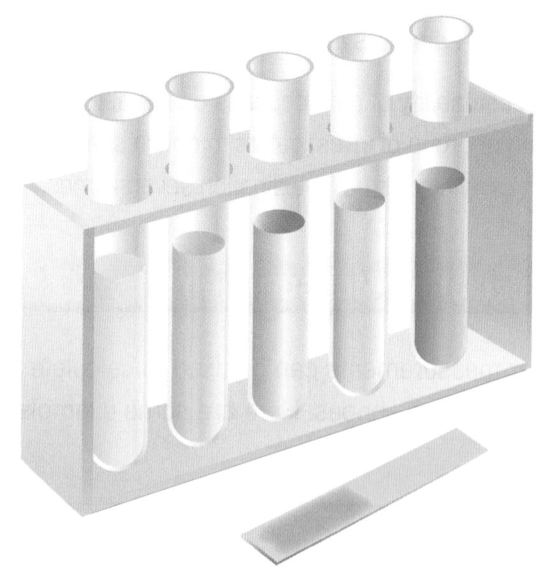

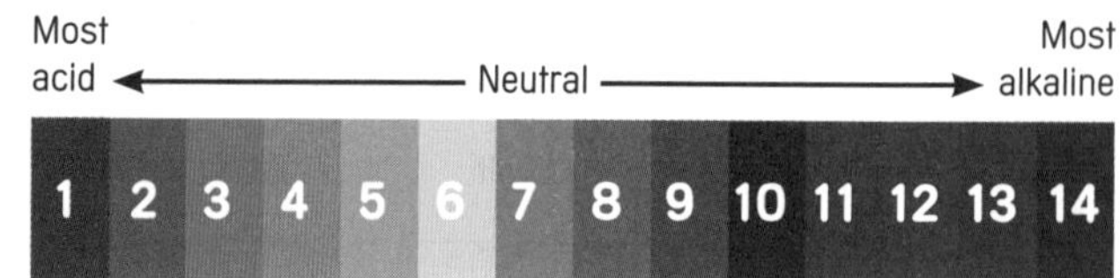

Assessing Water Quality

Water may be...

- pure
- contain dissolved solids, or
- contain suspended solids.

Suspended solids are particles that have a similar density to the water.

Particles denser than water settle to the bottom and form a **sediment**.

The **turbidity** of water is its cloudiness. It is caused by suspended solids, e.g....

- small particles such as mud and sand
- algae, bacteria and other microorganisms
- chemical precipitates.

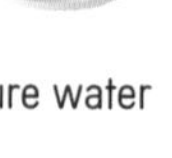

Pure water

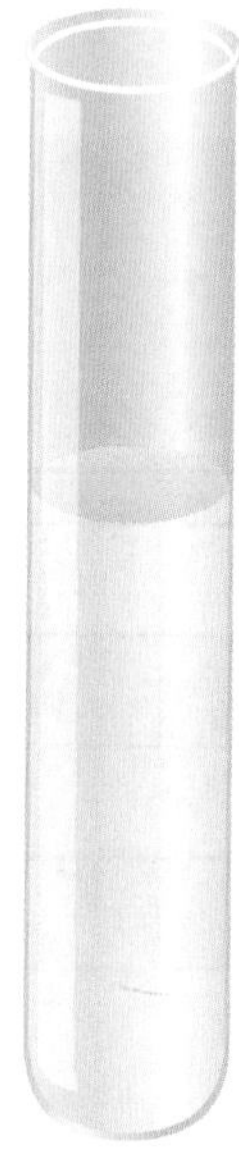

Water with dissolved solids. Liquid is a clear solution. Particles are ions or small molecules.

Water with suspended solids. Fine solid particles spread throughout the liquid.

Key Words Qualitative • Semi-quantitative • pH scale • Suspended solid • Sediment • Turbidity

Measuring Water Turbidity

Scientists use three methods to measure turbidity.

<table>
<tr>
<td>A turbidity tube is a glass tube with a black circle marked on the bottom.
1 Slowly add the water to be tested.
2 Continue to pour the water until the circle just disappears.
3 Take a reading.
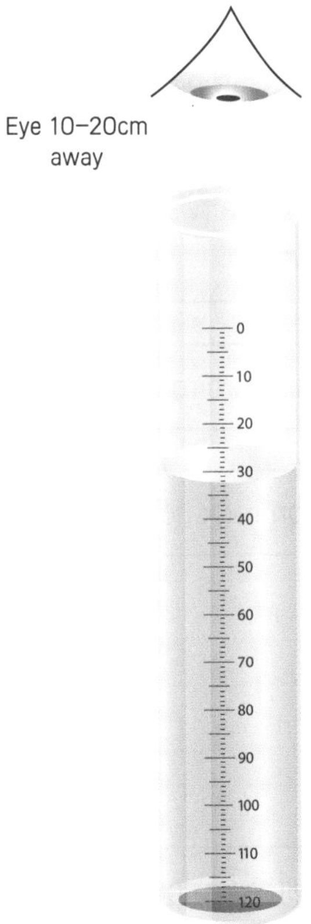
</td>
<td>A turbidity meter has a photoelectric cell that measures light scattered by particles in the sample.
1 Place the water sample in the turbidity meter.
2 Switch on. A light is shone through the sample.
3 Take a reading.
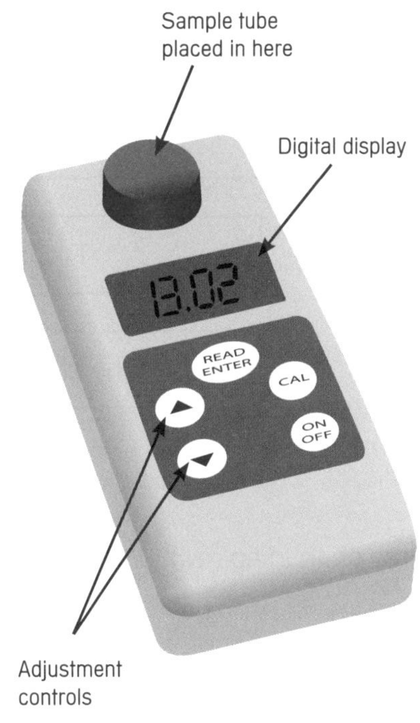
</td>
<td>A Secchi disc is a black and white disc, 20cm in diameter.
1 Lower the disc into the water until it can't be seen.
2 Record the depth (in metres).
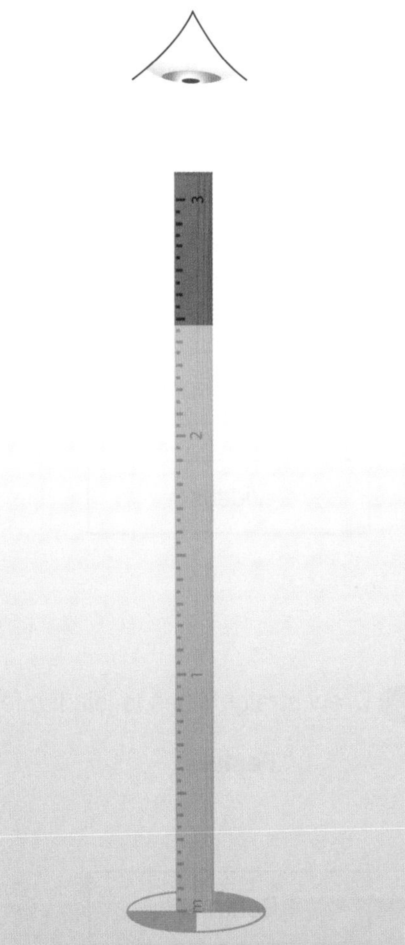</td>
</tr>
</table>

Quick Test

1. What colour is litmus in acid?
2. Are the following tests **qualitative**, **semi-quantitative** or **quantitative**?
   (a) Litmus **(b)** Universal indicator
3. What is the difference between dissolved solids and suspended solids?
4. Name **one** instrument used to measure the turbidity of water.

A3 Exam Practice Questions

1 Complete the following sentences. Use words from this list. **[2]**

common practice **representative** **proficiency** **accreditation** **health and safety**

The reliability and repeatability of evidence can be increased by using a system

of ....

A .... test involves a group of laboratories carrying out the same analysis.

2 Scientists use several methods to record different types of information. Draw straight lines to join the best **method of recording** with the **type of information** to be recorded. **[3]**

Method	Information to be recorded
Written description	A rough plan of an area marking sampling points
Drawing	The number and types of butterfly that visit different flowers over a week
Photographs	The feeding behaviour of a bird
Videos	The effects of an oil spill on rock pools

3 Draw straight lines to join the features of an image with the correct definitions. **[3]**

Feature	Definition
Contrast	Whether the image is blurred or not
Depth of field	A measure of how much bigger the image is than the object
Magnification	The extent to which objects at different distances from the camera are in focus
Sharpness of focus	The extent to which parts of an image are distinguishable from other objects and the background

4 **(a)** What is meant by the turbidity of a liquid? **[1]**

(b) Describe a method to measure the turbidity of an environmental water sample. **[4]**

5 Explain why environmental scientists investigating the effects of climate change study organisms found in the oceans.

The quality of written communication will be assessed in your answer to this question. **[6]**

HT **6** Complete the following table about error. **[4]**

	Definition	One Possible Cause
Random Error		
Systematic Error		

7 Draw straight lines to join the terms with the correct definitions. **[2]**

Term	Definition
Accuracy	How closely a number of measurements agree
Error	How close a measurement is to its true value
Precision	The difference between the measured value and its true value

A4 Scientists Protecting the Public

Scientific Experts

The work of scientific experts contributes to consumer health and safety and to law enforcement.

These practitioners must have good...

- scientific knowledge and understanding
- observational skills
- measurement skills
- analytical skills.

They must work carefully to avoid contamination of samples. Health and safety regulations affect the work they do. They must be able to work without causing harm to themselves, including in environments that they are called out to.

Consumer Protection

Public analysts check to see if health and safety standards are being met. Analysts need to have a good understanding of...

- chemical analysis
- the law
- the latest food technology.

Public analysts...

- check to see if health and safety standards are being met
- monitor food safety
- check labelling and compliance with legislation
- provide research and advice on diseases caused by food.

Law Enforcement

Crime scene investigators (CSIs) or **scenes of crime officers (SOCOs)** record, collect and package evidence found at crime scenes.

Their work may include...

- collecting fingerprints
- examining victims, suspects and locations for traces of **forensic** evidence, e.g. hairs, fibres, DNA.

Forensic scientists analyse the evidence collected at crime scenes by CSIs/SOCOs.

Forensic scientists are also involved in activities such as paternity testing.

Colorimetry

When a coloured chemical is dissolved in a liquid, the intensity of colour of the solution will increase as more of the chemical is added.

A **colorimeter** is an instrument used to measure the **intensity** of a colour. **Colorimetry** analyses colour in order to provide **quantitative** information.

You can use colorimeters to measure the **concentration** of a coloured chemical in a solution:

1. Select the colour filter to be used.
2. Pass light through a test tube of a colourless solvent and set the colorimeter to zero.
3. Pass light through standard reference coloured solutions of known concentration of a particular chemical. Record the absorbance values on the meter.
4. Plot the data to produce a **calibration graph** (absorbance against concentration).
5. Pass light through the unknown solution and compare its absorbance value with your plotted graph to find the concentration.

The darker the colour or more concentrated the solution, the higher the absorbance value.

The sensitivity of a colorimeter depends on the sensitivity of its photocell. The photocell receives light after it has passed through the sample. The light is monitored as either...

- absorbance
- percentage transmission.

The absorbance scale is the more sensitive scale.

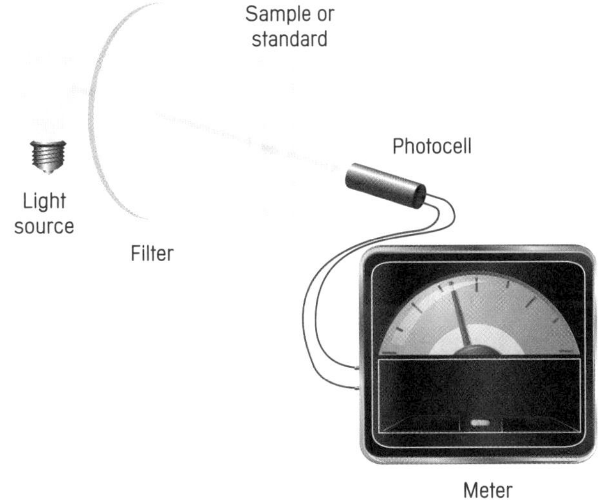

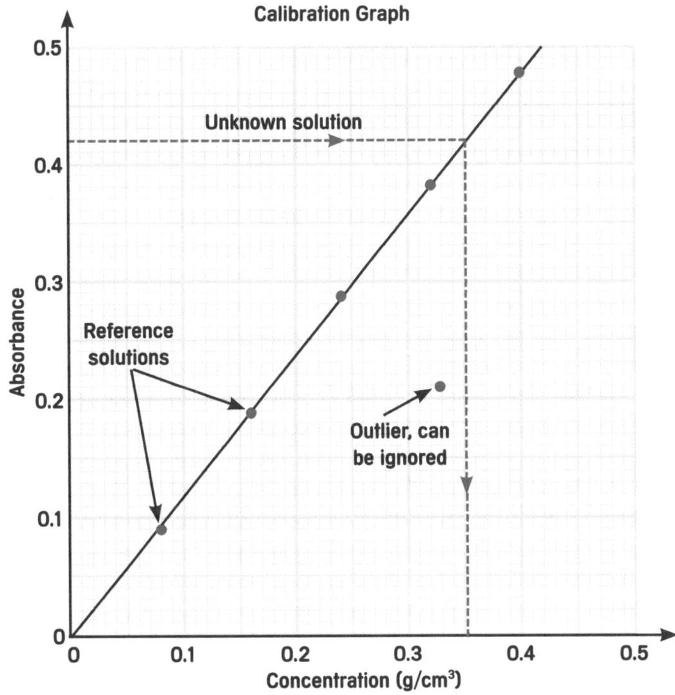

Quick Test

1. Is this statement **true** or **false**? Public analysts need a good understanding of the law and chemical analysis.
2. What does a CSI (or SOCO) do?
3. What instrument is used to measure the concentration of a coloured chemical in solution?
4. What is the name of the graph drawn by scientists when measuring the concentration of a coloured chemical in solution?

Key Words Colorimeter • Quantitative

A4 Scientists Protecting the Public

Light Microscopes

You can use a **light microscope** to look at an image in more detail. The microscope increases the **magnification** and **resolution** of the image.

The main parts of a compound light microscope and their functions are as follows:

- **Stage** – holds the slide.
- **Coarse focus** – moves the objective lens up and down to bring the image into focus.
- **Fine focus** – makes slight adjustments so that the detail of the image is clear.
- **Eyepiece lens** – where you look into the microscope.
- **Objective lens** – magnifies the specimen.
- **Slide** – a piece of glass used to hold the specimen.
- **Light source** – illuminates the specimen. (On some microscopes this is a mirror.)

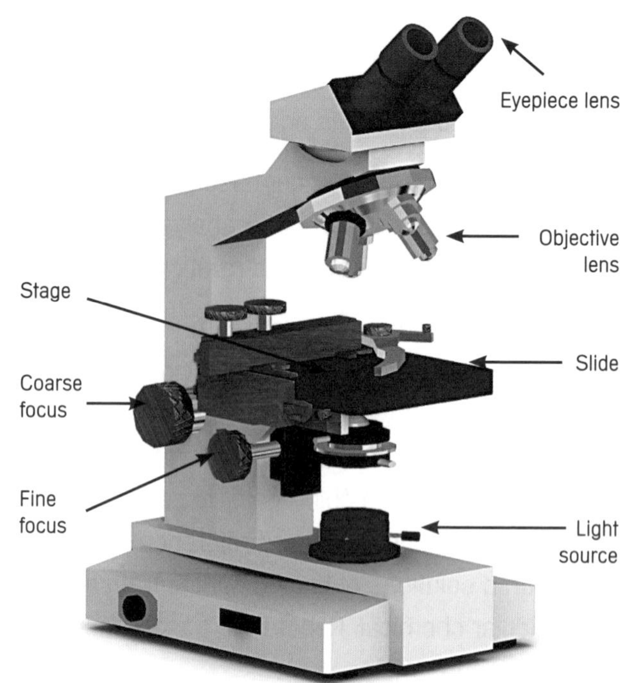

Magnification

You can calculate the **magnification** of a light microscope using the equation opposite.

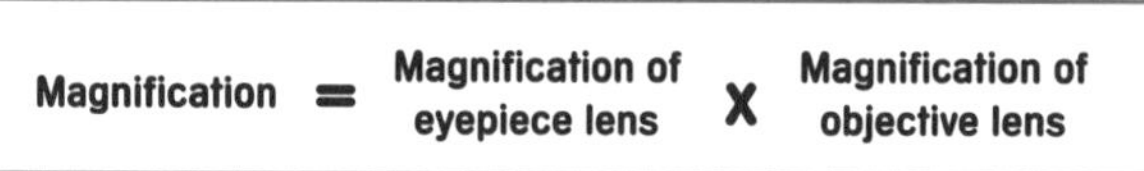

Magnification = Magnification of eyepiece lens x Magnification of objective lens

HT **Resolution** is the minimum distance required between two points in order for them to appear as separate points. A microscope with greater resolution allows you to see details that are very close together. The resolution of light microscopes is limited by the wavelength of light. It is unsuitable for transparent samples that are smaller than around a micrometre.

Depth of field is the range of distances within which a specimen is in focus. A light microscope has a **narrow** depth of field so objects just above or below the image area appear blurred. Microscopes have to be focused exactly on to the structure that's being examined.

Preparing Slides

The method used to prepare a light microscope slide depends on the sample.

Method 1: Blood Sample

1. Place a small drop of blood onto a clean slide.
2. Hold a second slide at an angle to the first one.
3. Pull the top slide back to touch the blood.
4. Push the top slide away to cause a smear.
5. Cover the sample with a cover slip.

Method 2: Hair Sample

1. Place one drop of glycerol onto a clean microscope slide.
2. Carefully place a short length of the hair on the slide using forceps.
3. Use a mounted needle to lower a cover slip over the hair.

Key Words Light microscope • Magnification • Resolution

Electron Microscopes

Electron microscopes use a beam of electrons instead of a beam of light.

Scanning electron microscopes (SEM) enable scientists to see greater surface detail of a specimen.

HT With an electron microscope, a much greater magnification is possible. They also have a greater **resolution** than light microscopes. Electrons in the beam are so tiny that they can pick out parts of an object that are very close together.

Depth of field refers to how much of the sample is in focus at the same time. Scanning electron microscopes have a wide depth of field.

If samples are poorly presented or poorly prepared, the image seen through an electron microscope will be poor.

Scanning Electron Microscope Image of Fungal Mycelium

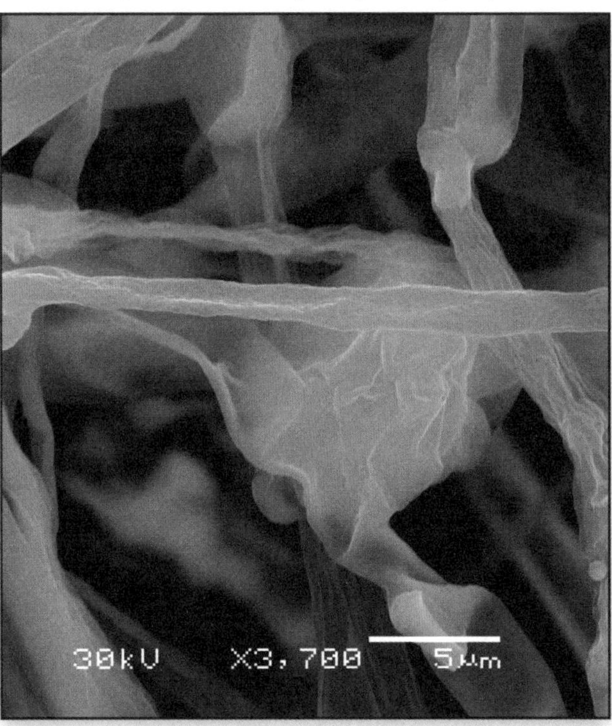

Comparing Microscopes

Method	Advantages	Disadvantages
Light microscopy	• Cheap • Portable • Samples can be prepared quickly for immediate results • Can observe living specimens	• Relatively low magnification • Relatively low resolution
Electron microscopy	• High magnification • High resolution	• Expensive to buy and run • Living organisms, cells or tissues have to be killed and preserved to be observed • Large and static • Samples take a long time to prepare

Quick Test

1. What is the magnification with a ×10 eyepiece lens and a ×40 objective lens?
2. What is the stage of a microscope used for?
3. Why do scientists use scanning electron microscopes?
4. HT What is the resolution of a microscope?
5. HT Compare the depth of field of a light microscope and a scanning electron microscope.

Key Words Electron microscope

Chromatography

Chromatography is a technique used to find out what unknown substances are made up of.

Paper chromatography has five main stages:

1. If the substance is solid, dissolve it in a liquid to form a solution.
2. Place a spot of the solution on the pencil line of a sheet of chromatography paper and allow to dry.
3. Place the bottom edge of the paper into a suitable **solvent** (e.g. water).
4. As the solvent rises up the paper, it dissolves the 'spot' and carries it up the paper.
5. The different chemicals in the solution separate, leaving marks on the paper.

Thin layer chromatography (TLC) uses a TLC plate instead of paper.

A TLC plate consists of a thin layer of powder (e.g. silica gel) coated onto a flat, unreactive surface (e.g. glass).

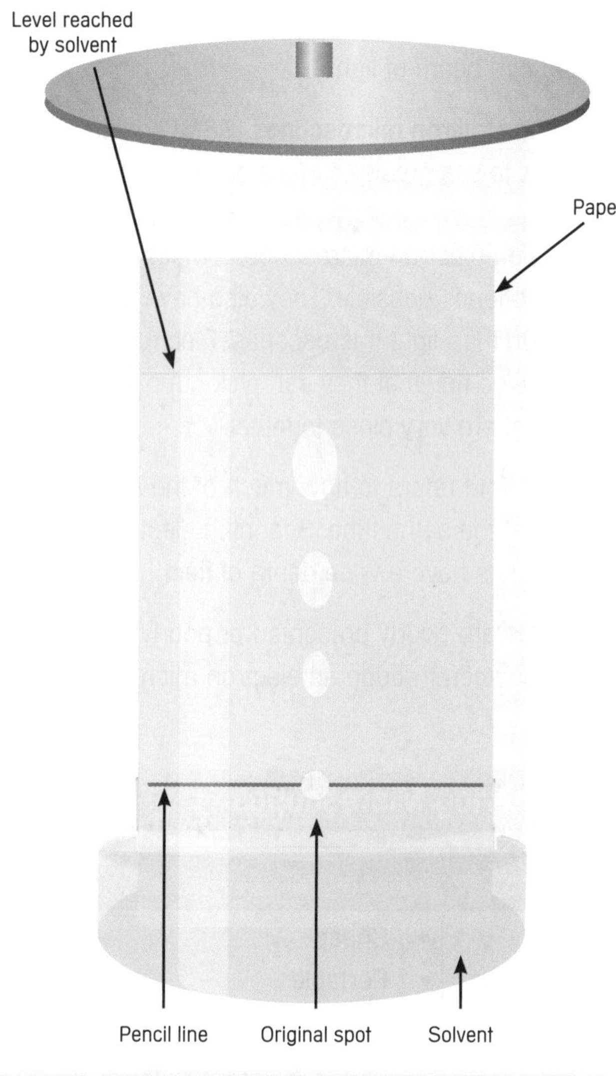

Chromatographic Phases

The solvent that's used to move the substance is the **mobile phase**.

The medium that it moves through (for example, paper) is called the **stationary phase**.

If the substance dissolves in water you can use water as the solvent. If it doesn't, you may be able to use a non-aqueous solvent to dissolve it.

Chromatography is the separation of chemicals as they move between the mobile phase and the stationary phase.

HT The chemical molecules in a substance travel different distances according to how strongly they're attracted to...

- the molecules in the stationary phase
- the solvent molecules.

Some chromatograms have to be **developed** to show the presence of colourless substances.

Sometimes, colourless spots can be viewed under ultraviolet (UV) light and marked on the paper/plate.

In other cases, it's necessary to spray the chromatogram with a chemical that causes the spots to become coloured.

Key Words Chromatography • Solvent • Mobile phase • Stationary phase

Using Chromatography

Chromatograms of known substances (**reference standards**) can be used to identify...

- an unknown substance
- separated chemicals of an unknown substance.

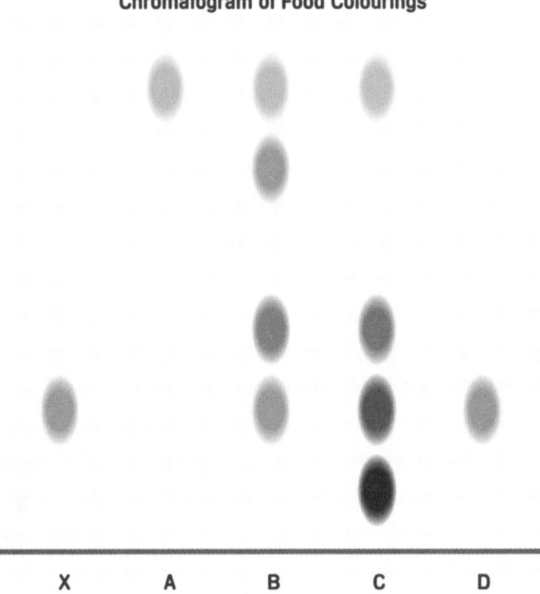

Comparing unknown food colouring X to known food colourings A, B, C and D, you can see that food colouring X is food colouring D.

The movement of a substance relative to the movement of the solvent is given by the **R_f value**.

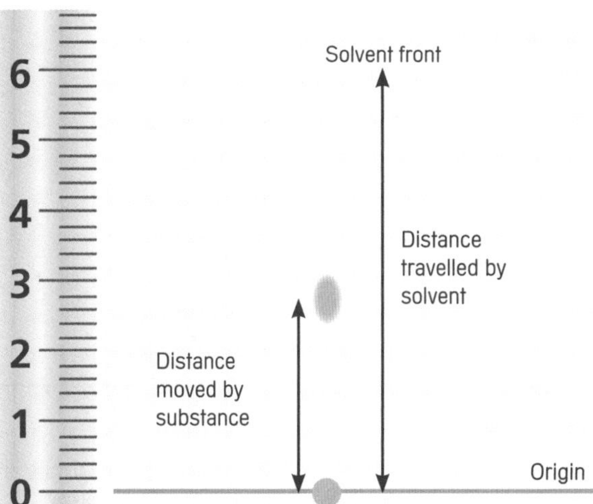

The R_f value can help you to identify the unknown substances.

To work out the R_f value, use the following formula:

$$R_f \text{ value} = \frac{\textbf{Distance travelled by substance}}{\textbf{Distance travelled by solvent}}$$

Using TLC

Thin layer chromatography has a number of advantages over paper chromatography even though they are similar processes.

As a result, TLC usually produces **better separations** for a wider range of substances.

Advantages of TLC include...

- TLC plates are easier to handle
- faster runs
- more even movement of the mobile phase through the stationary phase
- a choice of stationary phases
- results that are more easily reproduced.

TLC and paper chromatography are relatively **cheap** but have **limited uses**.

Quick Test

1. What is the mobile phase in chromatography?
2. Give **two** advantages of thin layer chromatography over paper chromatography.
3. What is a chromatogram of a known substance called?
4. What is done to a chromatogram of colourless substances to make them visible?
5. Write down the equation used to calculate the R_f value of a substance.
6. HT The distance a substance moves on a chromatogram depends on **two** factors. What are these?

Key Words R_f value

HT Two-way Chromatography

When scientists separate mixtures, sometimes the chemicals in the mixture have very similar, or identical, R_f values.

To separate these, scientists can use a technique called **two-way chromatography**.

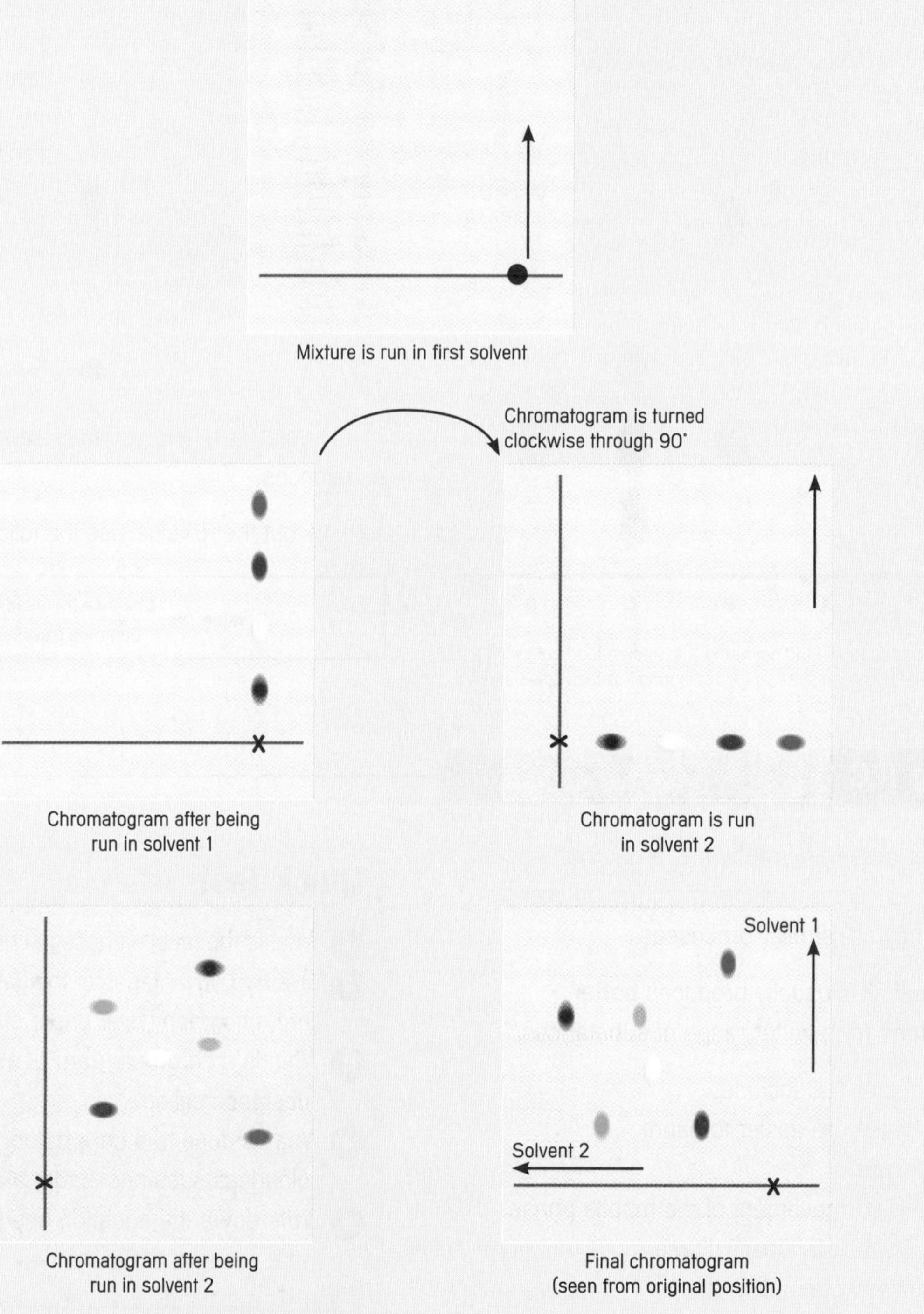

Mixture is run in first solvent

Chromatogram after being run in solvent 1

Chromatogram is run in solvent 2

Chromatogram after being run in solvent 2

Final chromatogram (seen from original position)

In the example, the first solvent suggested that there are four chemicals in the mixture.

Two-way chromatography has shown that there are six chemicals in it.

Key Words Two-way chromatography

Electrophoresis

Electrophoresis is a technique used to separate different biological molecules, such as proteins. It can be used...

- on small biological samples
- for scientific detection, such as producing **DNA** profiles.

DNA profiling uses gel electrophoresis and can be used...

- to place people at a crime scene and therefore help solve crimes (including old crimes – 'cold cases')
- in paternity testing.

HT Electrophoresis separates components in a mixture because their particles carry different charges.

Electrophoresis involves the following stages:

1. The sample is placed onto an absorbent material, e.g. a gel.
2. A charge is passed across the absorbent material.
3. Negative particles move towards the positive electrode. Positive particles move towards the negative electrode.

The separation and distance travelled depends on the size of the molecule and the charge. Small molecules with large charges travel the furthest.

Gel Electrophoresis

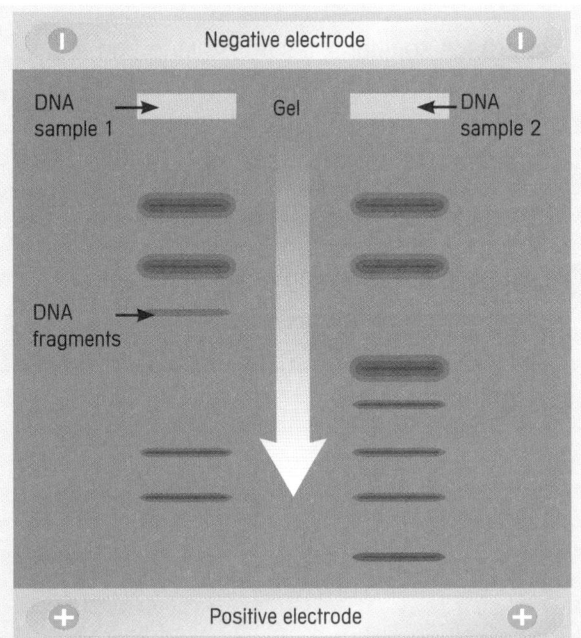

Quick Test

1. What is the name of the technique used to produce a DNA profile?
2. Give **one** example of a use of DNA profiling.
3. What is a DNA database?
4. How does the polymerase chain reaction (PCR) improve DNA profiling?
5. HT During the production of a DNA profile, which electrode do negative particles move towards?

Improving Technology

Developments in DNA profiling technology improve its use in law enforcement.

Examples include the following:

1. The polymerase chain reaction (PCR). This...
   - produces many identical copies of the DNA sample (**amplifies** the DNA)
   - allows tiny amounts of DNA to be analysed.
2. DNA databases
   - These contain DNA profiles of people connected with crimes committed.
   - They are stored on the UK's National DNA Database.
   - They allow forensic scientists to make quick, accurate and reliable comparisons of DNA samples.
   - Some people object to DNA profiles being stored for long periods of time after the crime has been committed for ethical reasons.

Key Words Electrophoresis • DNA

A4 Exam Practice Questions

1 Complete the following sentences. Use words from this list. **[3]**

absorbance **calibration** **concentration** **quantity** **solution** **standard** **transmission**

Colorimeters will give a scientist quantitative data. By using ....

reference solutions, it's possible to find the .... of a coloured chemical

in a ....

Colorimeters have two scales: .... and .... Using the

data obtained, scientists draw a .... graph.

2 Complete the following table on the advantages and disadvantages of light and electron microscopy. **[4]**

Microscopy	Advantages	Disadvantages
Light microscopy	1. .... 2.	1. .... 2. ....
Electron microscopy	1. .... 2.	1. .... 2. ....

3 For each piece of evidence, **(a)–(c)**, choose the most appropriate method of analysis from this list. Explain why each method is the most appropriate.

Light microscopy **Paper / Thin layer chromatography** **Colorimetry**

Fingerprinting **Electrophoresis**

(a) The types of dye in a coloured sample extracted from food. **[1]**

....

....

(b) A sample of blood that could be from either the victim or a suspect. **[1]**

....

....

(c) A sample of hair that could have been shed, pulled or cut. **[1]**

....

....

4 Chromatography can be used to analyse unknown substances. Write down definitions of the following terms used in chromatography.

(a) Mobile phase **[1]**

(b) Stationary phase **[1]**

(c) Developer **[1]**

5 Give and describe an example where changes in technology have improved methods of law enforcement.

The quality of written communication will be assessed in your answer to this question. **[6]**

HT 6 Describe how a scanning electron microscope provides images of a greater detail than light microscopy. **[2]**

B1 Sports Equipment

People and Organisations

Companies and people working in the production of sports equipment need a good knowledge and understanding of materials and their properties.

People working in the production of sports equipment include...

- the equipment designer
- the equipment manufacturer
- the equipment tester.

Practitioners in this area need a good knowledge and understanding of...

- the science of materials and their properties
- how to analyse the properties of materials, and what their analyses mean
- the features items of sports equipment needed to make it perform well.

They must follow health and safety regulations carefully when handling and testing materials and sports equipment.

Choosing Materials

Designers and manufacturers of sports equipment must be able to select the correct material for each job.

When choosing a material you should take into account factors including...

- durability
- cost
- environmental impact
- appearance
- other specific properties, e.g. strength.

Materials are classified by their properties. The properties of materials are determined by their **internal (atomic or molecular) structures**.

The main classes of materials are...

- **metals and alloys**, e.g. copper, steel
- **polymers**, e.g. polythene, Kevlar®
- **ceramics**, e.g. glass, porcelain
- **composites**, e.g. carbon fibre, fibreglass
- **woods and wood products**, e.g. willow, MDF.

Maintaining and Enforcing Standards

Standards are set for different types of products to ensure safety, quality and consistency.

Organisations that set product standards include...

- the **British Standards Institution (BSI)**
- the **European Committee for Standardization (CEN)**
- the **International Organization for Standardization (ISO)**.

CE Mark (CEN)

CE

Only products that meet an organisation's standards can display their symbols, e.g. the BSI Kitemark.

Certain practitioners make sure that products have been designed within **safety margins**. For example...

- trading standards officers might inspect sportswear and equipment to check on manufacturing standards, its safety for use and the effects of wear and tear
- building control surveyors inspect new buildings, e.g. a new leisure centre, to check they're well constructed.

HT Traceability

Regularly checking equipment ensures that scientists know the accuracy of measurements they make.

Measurements made with devices must be compared with reference standards with known accuracy. These begin with checks within a laboratory or manufacturing company and end with checks against international standards.

Each comparison is a link in a **chain** of comparisons.

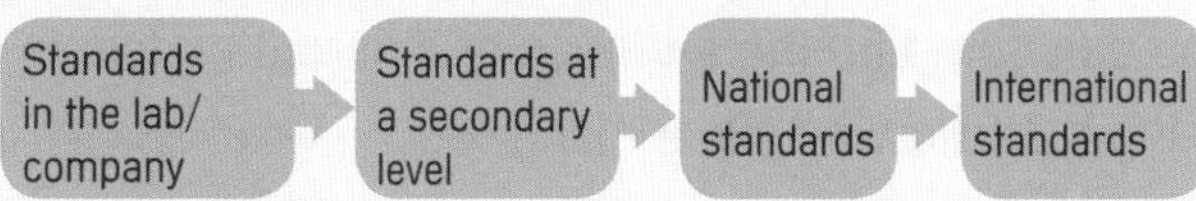

For standards to be maintained, laboratories should be able to demonstrate that this chain of checks against standards is in place and unbroken. This is called **traceability**.

National standards bodies, such as the National Physical Laboratory (NPL), check standards.

Mechanical Behaviour of Materials

The mechanical properties of a material are described using the following terms:

- **Stiffness/flexibility**
  - How resistant a material is to bending. A material with a high stiffness isn't very flexible.
  - Made from stiff materials: racket handles, oars, bicycle frames.
- **Toughness/brittleness**
  - How resistant a material is to snapping. Tough materials aren't very brittle.
  - Made from tough materials: rackets, bicycle frames, snowboards, blades used for fencing.
- **Density**
  - How heavy a certain volume of material is. The denser a material is, the greater the mass of a standard volume.
  - Made from low density materials: bicycle frames.
  - Made from high density materials: bowls.
- **Tensile strength** (i.e. breaking strength)
  - Measures the force needed to break a material loaded under **tension**.
  - Made from material with great tensile strength: cables in gym equipment, ropes for climbing, tennis racket strings.
- **Compressive strength**
  - Measures the force a material can withstand before fracturing when loaded under **compression**.
  - Made from materials with great compressive strength: golf balls, cricket balls, helmets, boat hulls.
- **Hardness**
  - Hard materials are more difficult to scratch than soft materials.
  - Made from hard materials: ice skate blades.
- **Durability**
  - The ability to resist wear and tear.
  - Made from durable materials: shoes, goggles.

Quick Test

1. Name **two** organisations that set product standards.
2. What term is used to describe a material that is resistant to wear?
3. HT Name the term used to describe a chain of comparisons with measurement standards.

Key Words Traceability • Tensile strength • Compressive strength • Durability

Measuring Stiffness

You can compare the **stiffness** of different materials using the following experiment:

1. Support the material to be tested with a clamp at each end.
2. Gradually add masses onto the middle of the material.
3. The masses will cause the material to **bend**.
4. Record the mass needed to produce a fixed amount of bending.
5. Repeat the test with different materials. (They must all have the same dimensions.)
6. The material that needs the greatest mass to make it bend the fixed amount is the stiffest.

You can also use a similar method where the material is clamped at one end and masses are applied to the opposite end.

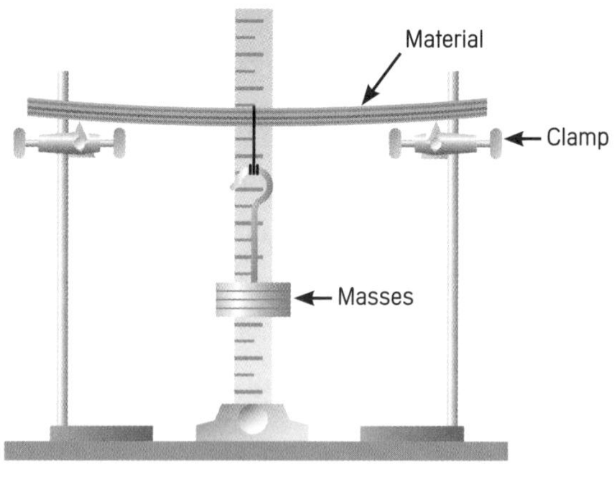

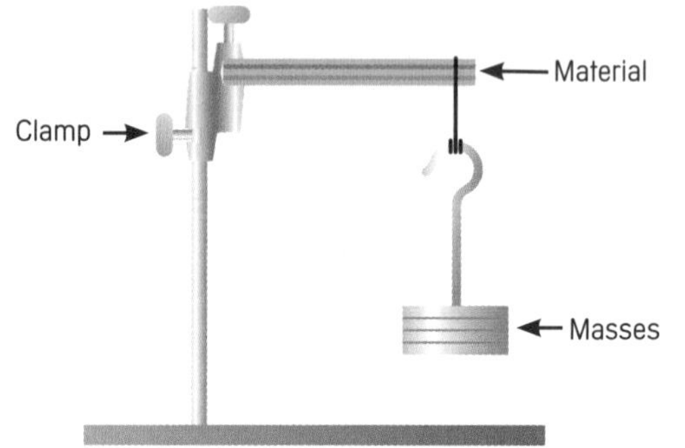

Measuring Tensile Strength

You can compare the **tensile strength** of different materials using the following experiment:

1. Stretch a piece of the material to be tested between a clamp and a pulley wheel.
2. Add masses onto the end of the material to increase the stretching force.
3. When the breaking strain of the material is reached it will **snap**.
4. Record the mass needed to snap the material.
5. Repeat the test with different materials. (They must all have the same dimensions.)
6. The material that needs the greatest mass to make it snap has the greatest tensile strength.

You can use a similar method to measure the extension of a material as a force is applied to it (measure its new length as masses are added).

Tensile Strength Testing Equipment

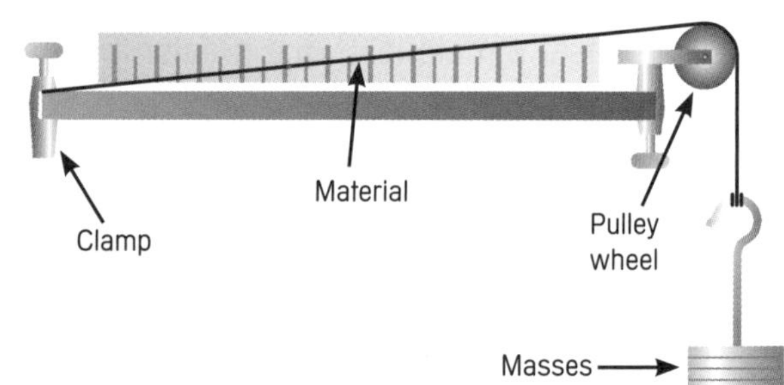

 Key Words Tensile strength

HT Elastic and Plastic Behaviour

When a force is applied to a material it can show either of the following;

- **Elastic behaviour** – the material springs back to its original shape when the force is removed.
- **Plastic behaviour** – the material doesn't return to its original shape when the force is removed (because the force is too great).

Force–Extension Graphs

A **force–extension graph** shows how a material stretches when it's under **tensile** stress.

HT You can use force–extension graphs to predict the elastic and plastic behaviour of a material.

In the example graph...

- the material displays **elastic behaviour** over the **straight**-line section
- after the 'elastic limit' the graph **curves**, showing that the material is displaying **plastic behaviour**.

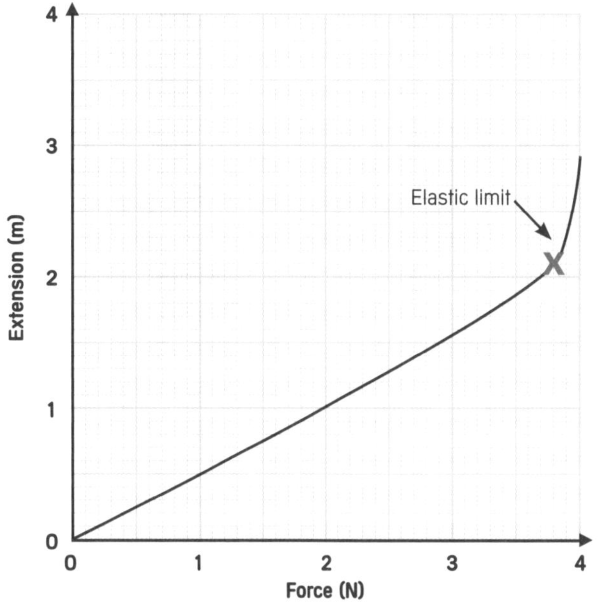

Stored Energy

The **area** under a force–extension graph is equal to the **energy** (in J) stored in a stretched sample.

HT As long as the elastic limit hasn't been reached, the extension for any given force can be predicted using the formula opposite.

N.B. The gradient of the graph is the spring constant (k).

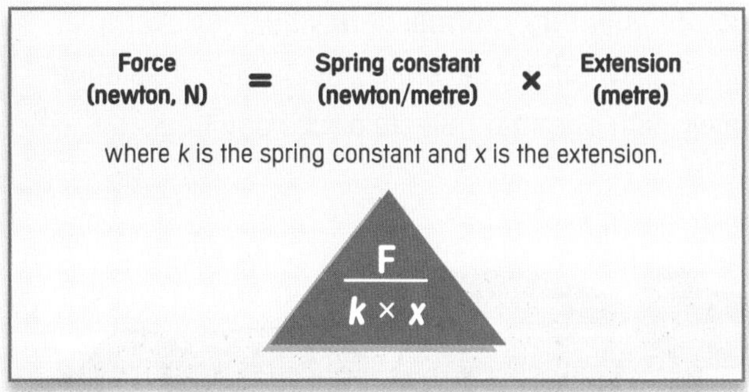

Force (newton, N) = Spring constant (newton/metre) × Extension (metre)
where *k* is the spring constant and *x* is the extension.
F
k × x

B1 Sports Equipment

Thermal Properties of Materials

The **thermal conductivity** of a material describes how easy it is for heat to flow through it.

At the same temperature, a material with a low thermal conductivity will feel warmer than one with a high thermal conductivity. This is because when you touch a material with a high thermal conductivity, the heat from your hand easily passes through the material.

Copper – high thermal conductance

Wood – low thermal conductance

Thermal conductivity can determine which materials are best suited to a specific purpose. Materials with low thermal conductance will be insulating. They are used in sportswear such as skiwear and wet suits.

The **thermal reflectivity** of a material describes how easily heat is reflected by the material. In some skiwear, a layer of material is used to reflect back body heat, helping to keep the body warm.

Using Thermal Properties

When designing a product, you might select materials for their **matching thermal properties**. For example, the piston and cylinders in the engine of a car need to expand at the same rate.

Alternatively, you might select materials for their **complementary thermal behaviour**. For example, some skiwear has layers combining an insulating layer with one that reflects back body heat.

Key Words Thermal conductivity • Thermal reflectivity

Using the Right Materials

The suitability of materials for making sports equipment depends on their properties.

Material	Properties
Metals and alloys	• good **conductors of electricity** and heat • shiny • stiff • ductile (can be drawn out into a wire) • malleable (can be hammered into shape)
Polymers	• insulators of electricity and heat • low density • often flexible • often plastic
Ceramics	• insulators of heat and electricity • low density • stiff • brittle

HT It's often the **combination of properties** that makes a material suitable for a job. For example, **carbon fibres** are used for making bicycle frames because they're light and strong.

Often, different materials with complementary properties are used.

You might choose to select materials for their **complementary mechanical behaviour**.

For example...

- cycle helmets (force-spreading outer shell; energy-absorbing inner lining)
- sports shoe (flexible outer layer; inner to support the foot).

Quick Test

1. What term is used to describe how quickly heat passes through a material?
2. Give **three** properties of metals.
3. What type of material is an insulator of heat, has a low density and is brittle?
4. What does ductile mean?
5. HT What is meant when a material shows plastic behaviour?
6. HT How would you use a force–extension graph to predict elastic and plastic behaviour?

Key Words

Conductor of electricity

B1 Sports Equipment

Improving Mechanical Properties

An **alloy** is made by mixing molten metal with other elements (often other metals). The elements in the mixture dissolve. When the mixture cools it forms a solid.

The benefit of using an alloy over a pure metal is that specific properties can be enhanced in the alloy.

For example...

- hardness
- tensile strength
- melting point
- resistance to corrosion.

Composite Materials

A **composite material** is made from more than one material. Usually, it has one material embedded into another, e.g. fibres set in a resin. The two most common composites are...

- fibreglass composites (used in boat hulls)
- carbon-fibre composites (used in Formula One cars).

Concrete is a composite used in the construction of sports buildings. It's made up of small stones called aggregate, embedded in a sand and cement mix. Concrete has a high compressive strength.

Laminated materials, e.g. laminated woods such as plywood, used in sports equipment such as skateboards and for building some canoes, are also composites.

The Structure of Composites

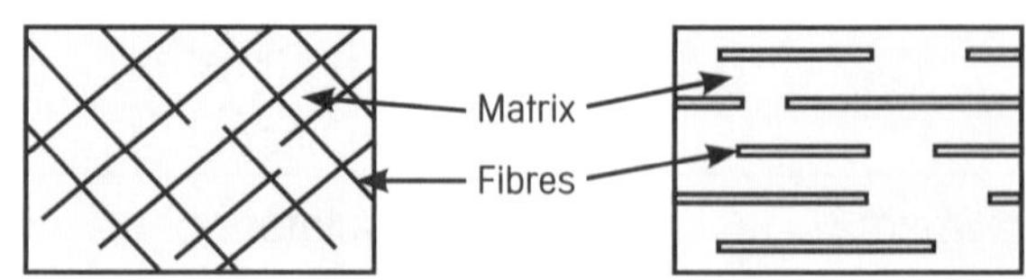

Plywood

HT Composite materials combine the useful properties of different materials while avoiding their drawbacks.

Fibreglass is a composite of glass and resin. The glass provides stiffness and the resin makes the composite tough and lightweight.

Kevlar® is a polymer used in many composite materials. It's used to add strength, toughness and durability. For example it's used in carbon-fibre and graphite tennis rackets, or with a low density polymer (e.g. polycarbonate) in cycle helmets.

Key Words Alloy • Composite material

Improving Sports Equipment

One way to improve sports equipment is to improve its mechanical properties.

Well-designed new equipment can have...

- increased strength and stiffness
- reduced density.

A product can be made more **rigid** by...

- changing the shape or increasing the thickness of the material
- using stronger or stiffer materials
- changing the structure.

Before a material is used to make a product, several factors need to be **evaluated** including...

- properties
- cost
- durability
- environmental impact
- appearance.

Development of New Materials

As new materials are developed, their use in sports equipment has improved sporting performance. For example...

- the piezoelectric materials in smart skis. Piezoelectric materials turn mechanical energy into electrical energy. Skis made with piezoelectric materials ('smart skis') dampen vibrations when skiing
- scandium-aluminium alloys in bicycle frames and baseball bats. Scandium-aluminium alloys combine strength with low density
- tennis racket frames are often made from carbon-fibre resin composites that give a high stiffness to mass ratio. The latest smart materials in tennis rackets control vibrations when hitting the ball and give control when hitting a hard or soft shot
- 'smart' two-core golf balls have a less dense, softer inner core and a high-density, high-compression outer core, to give the best performance on different types of shot.

Quick Test

1. What is a composite material?
2. How is an alloy made?
3. Is this statement **true** or **false**? Composite materials include fibreglass and plywood.

B1 Exam Practice Questions

1 What is the name of the quality standards mark of...

(a) the British Standards Institution? .... **[1]**

(b) the European Committee for Standardization? .... **[1]**

2 Which are properties of ceramics? Put ticks (✓) in the boxes next to the **two** correct options. **[2]**

Malleable	☐	Good conductors of heat and electricity	☐
Brittle	☐	Insulators of heat and electricity	☐

3 **(a)** What is tensile strength? **[1]**

....

....

(b) What is compressive strength? **[1]**

....

....

4 Give **three** ways in which a piece of sports equipment could be made more rigid. **[3]**

....

....

....

5 Describe how to measure the stiffness of a sample in the lab. **[5]**

....

....

....

....

....

....

....

6 Why can different materials at the same temperature feel warm or cold when touched? **[3]**

....

....

....

....

7 Draw straight lines to join the properties with the correct definitions. **[3]**

Property	**Definition**
Stiffness	The resistance of a material to wear
Tensile strength	The resistance of a material to bending
Durability	How resistant a material is to snapping
Toughness	How much force is needed to break a material when stretched

8 List **three** factors that need to be evaluated before a material is used to make sports equipment. **[3]**

HT 9 **(a)** What does a force–extension graph show? **[1]**

(b) A spring has a spring constant of 50N/m. There is a force of 4N acting on the spring. Calculate its extension. **[2]**

10 What is the difference between elastic and plastic behaviour? **[2]**

11 For a named example of a composite material, explain why the composite is a more suitable material to make sports equipment with than the materials that make up the composite.

The quality of written communication will be assessed in your answer to this question. **[6]**

Stage and Screen Productions

Many different organisations use sound and lighting effects, including...

- theatres
- film companies
- concert venues
- dance clubs.

Qualified practitioners are essential to stage and screen productions. They include...

- stage managers
- sound and lighting designers
- sound and lighting technicians and engineers
- visual and special effects experts.

Practitioners of stage and screen need a knowledge and understanding of...

- the science of sound and/or light and how to use these to maximum effect
- materials that reflect or absorb sound or light.

They need to be aware of the health and safety regulations required to...

- handle electrical equipment safely, in the studio, dance club, theatre or on location, and regularly check its safe working
- know about the hazards when using sound and different light sources, and the risks to both themselves and the public, and how to minimise these risks.

Light Sources

Useful light sources for film or stage include...

- sunlight
- incandescent lamps
- fluorescent lamps
- lasers.

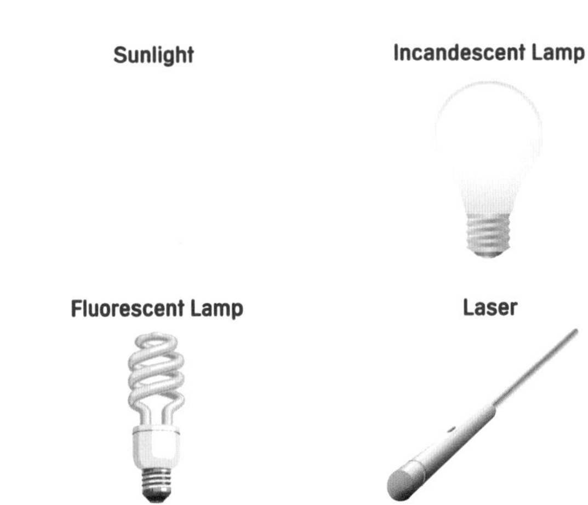

Some light sources emit unwanted **radiation**, for example:

- **Ultraviolet radiation (UV)**
  - Emitted by the Sun (along with visible light and infrared radiation).
  - Small amounts are emitted by compact fluorescent lights (low energy light bulbs) and UV lasers.
  - UV radiation can cause skin cancer.
- **Infrared radiation (IR)**
  - Most of the electromagnetic radiation emitted by incandescent lamps is infrared.
  - IR radiation causes heating.

Filters

White light is a combination of all the parts of the spectrum that make up visible light. The seven colours of the spectrum are red, orange, yellow, green, blue, indigo and violet. We can make white light by mixing three coloured lights:

- Blue
- Green
- Red.

A **filter** is a piece of glass or plastic that alters the colour, or nature, of a light source by absorbing some colours (blue, green, red), or other parts of the spectrum (UV, IR).

You need to know how white light appears when colours are removed.

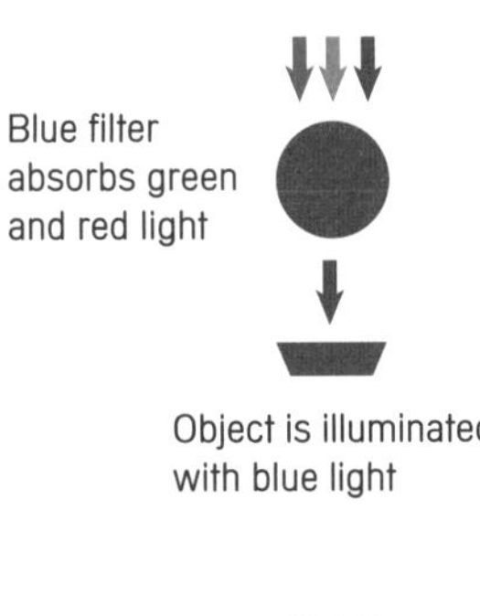

Blue filter absorbs green and red light

Object is illuminated with blue light

Green filter absorbs red and blue light

Object is illuminated with green light

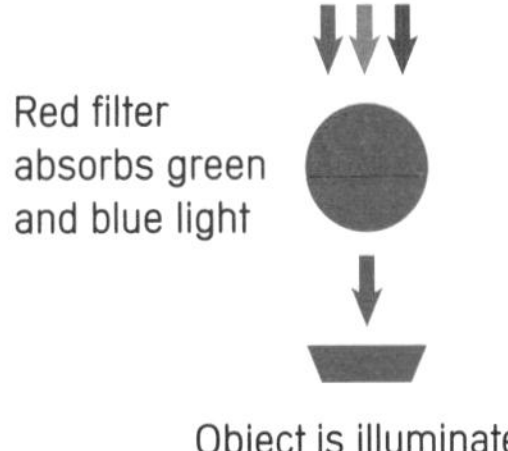

Red filter absorbs green and blue light

Object is illuminated with red light

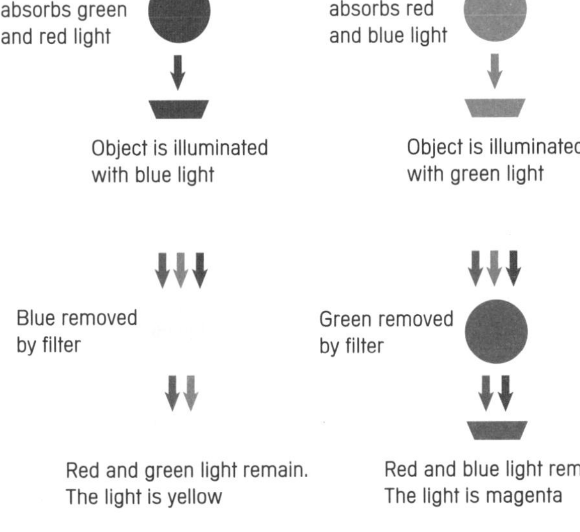

Blue removed by filter

Red and green light remain. The light is yellow

Green removed by filter

Red and blue light remain. The light is magenta

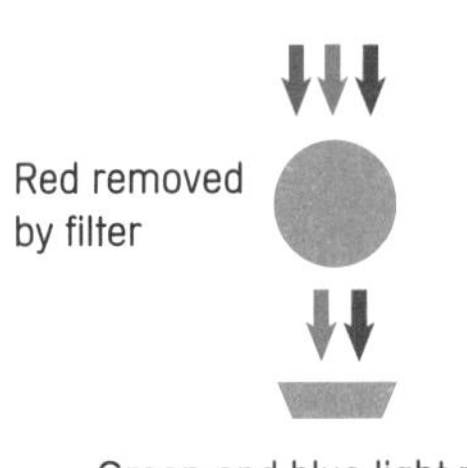

Red removed by filter

Green and blue light remain. The light is cyan

Quick Test

1. Name a natural source of ultraviolet radiation.
2. What is a filter?
3. What three colours can be mixed to produce white light?
4. What colour would you remove from white light to make it appear magenta?

Key Words Ultraviolet radiation • Infrared radiation • Filter

Optical Behaviour

To accurately describe the optical behaviour of a material you need to know the following terms:

- **Transparent** – lets light pass through virtually unchanged.
- **Reflective** – a surface that light bounces off.
- **Translucent** – lets light pass through, but scatters it. You can't see details through a translucent material.
- **Opaque** – doesn't let light pass through.
- **Refraction** – light passing from one material to another changes direction as it crosses the boundary between the materials. This is because light travels at different speeds in different materials.

N.B. Coloured glass isn't translucent. It's transparent to the colour it lets through and opaque to other colours.

HT The **refractive index** of a material is a measure of how much it bends light rays.

A material with a high refractive index bends light more towards the normal than a material with a lower refractive index.

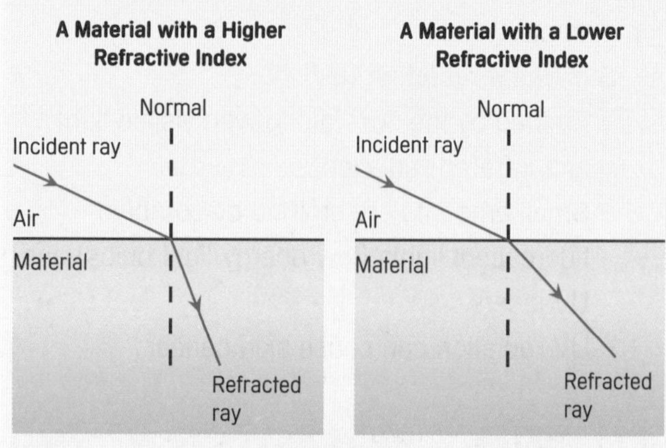

Mirrors

Light is reflected back from a mirror.

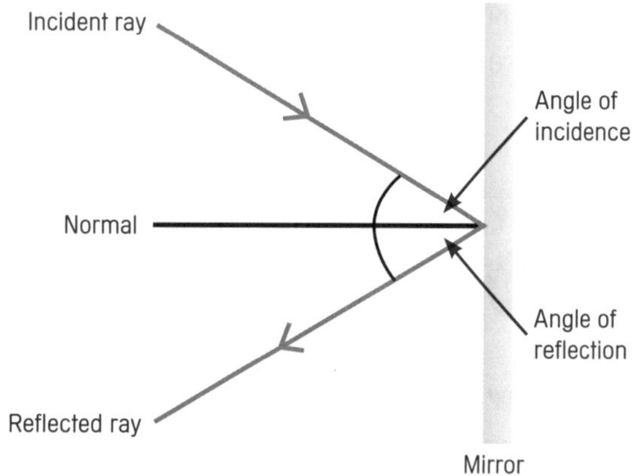

Characteristics of images formed by plane mirrors:

- The image is upright.
- The image has left and right reversed.
- The image is the same size as the object.

The image formed by a plane mirror is called a **virtual image**. The image appears to come from behind the mirror.

Another characteristic of a image formed by a plane mirror is that the image is the same distance behind the mirror as the object is in front of the mirror.

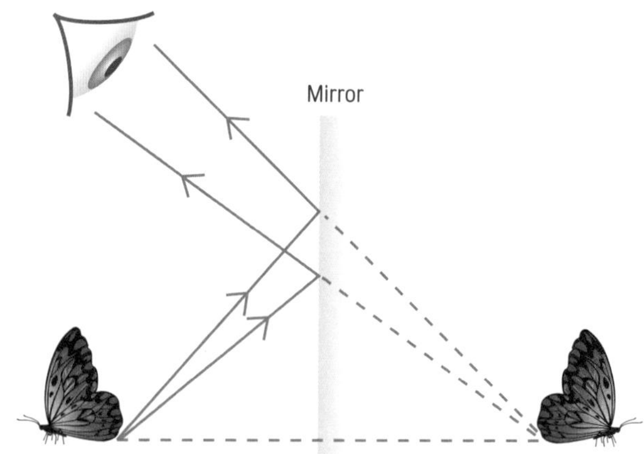

The image appears to be formed behind the mirror

Light rays from a distant object will be parallel. They will be reflected in the same way, and the image will appear to be formed behind the mirror.

Key Words Transparent • Reflective • Translucent • Opaque • Refraction • Virtual image

Lenses

Most lenses are made out of glass but some polymers (plastics) can also be used.

Light can be partially reflected at the surface of glass. To prevent this reflection occurring in cameras, a special coating is added to the lens. The coating allows more light to be transmitted through it.

Rays of light coming from a distant object are effectively **parallel**. Lenses are shaped to alter the behaviour of light rays in different ways.

A **diverging lens** is **concave**. It causes rays of light passing through it to spread out.

A **converging lens** is **convex**. It bends rays of light inwards, focusing an **image** of the object in the **focal plane**. The distance from the lens to the focal plane is called the **focal length**.

The power of a lens is measured in **dioptres**.

A more powerful lens will...
- have a shorter focal length
- focus the image closer to the lens.

Diverging Lens

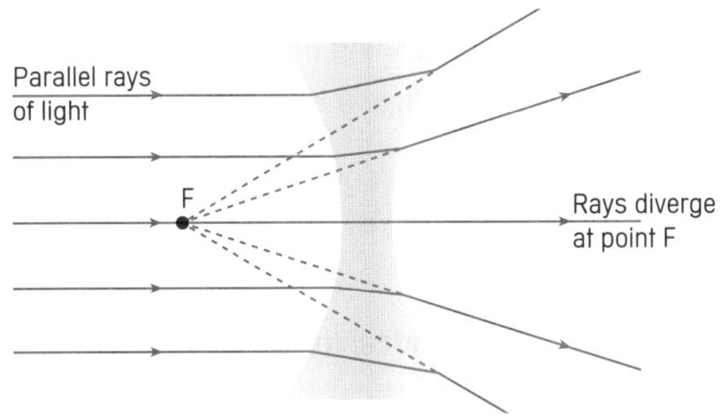

Converging Lens

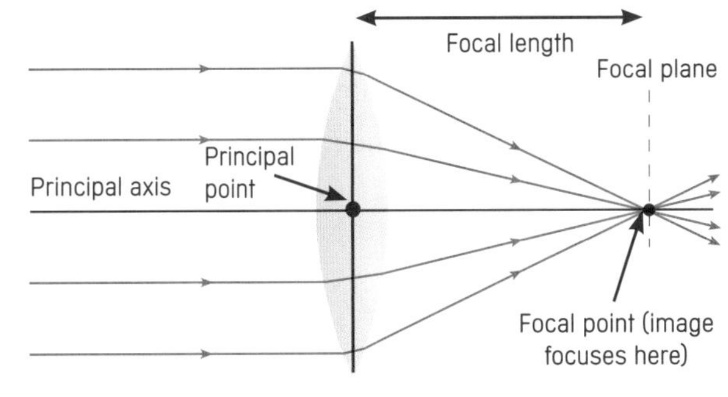

Cameras

A simple camera works in a similar way to the human eye. You should be able to identify the different parts of a camera:
- **Lens** – focuses the light from the object.
- **Shutter** – prevents light from entering the camera; opens to expose the film or image sensor when a picture is taken.
- **Aperture** – controls the amount of light entering when the shutter is opened.
- **Focal plane** – the film or image sensor is here and the image is focused on it.
- **Viewfinder** – shows what the photo will look like.

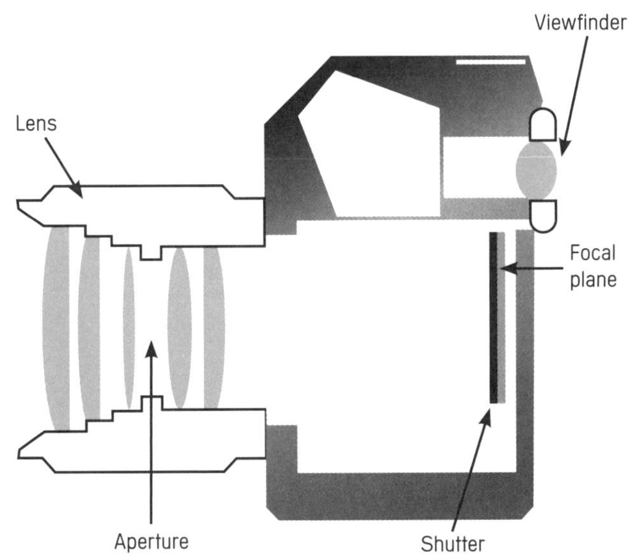

Key Words Diverging lens • Converging lens • Image • Focal plane • Focal length

B2 Stage and Screen

HT Refraction and Focus

A lens works because light rays **refract** when they enter and leave the surface of the lens. You can change the degree of refraction by altering the **curvature** of the lens. A greater curve will produce a shorter focal length.

When a distant object is moved closer to a camera or the eye, the image...

- becomes larger
- moves beyond the focal length.

To keep an image in focus, your eye makes the lens fatter. This...

- makes the lens more curved
- decreases the focal length.

Cameras maintain focus by moving the lens towards the object (away from the film or image sensor).

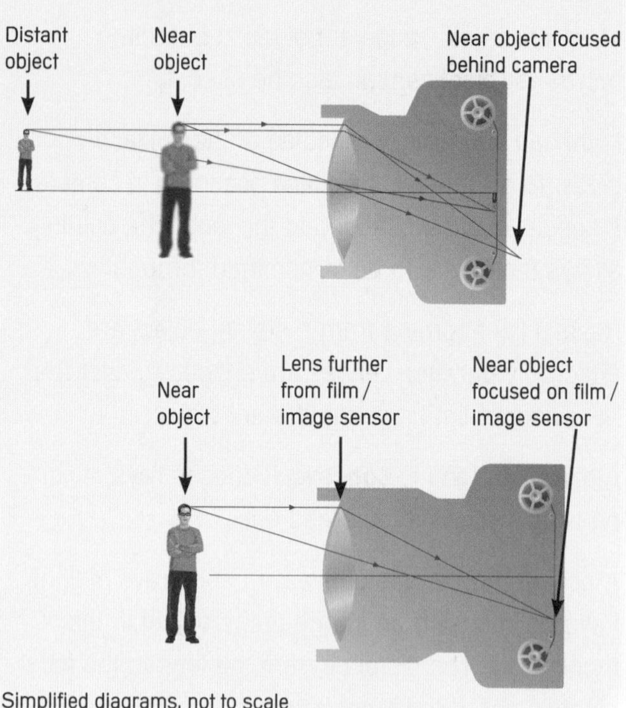

Simplified diagrams, not to scale

Describing Images

You should be able to describe an image using the following terms:

- **Real** – a **real image** is formed when rays of light actually meet (i.e. can be focused on a screen). Converging lenses form real images (except when the object is placed within the focal length of the lens – the lens then acts as a magnifying glass).
- **Virtual** – a **virtual image** is where rays of light appear to come from the image (i.e. can't be focused on a screen). Diverging lenses form virtual images.
- **Inverted** – upside down.
- **Upright** – the right way up.

You should also state whether an image is larger / smaller / the same size as the object.

The table shows the characteristics of images produced by common optical devices.

Device	Image Characteristics
Eye	Real, inverted and smaller than object
Camera	Real, inverted and smaller than object
Projector	Real, upright and larger than object
Magnifying glass	Virtual, upright and larger than object

Quick Test

1. What is the opposite of opaque?
2. What is meant by a translucent material?
3. What type of image is produced by...
   (a) a converging lens? **(b)** a diverging lens?
4. What shape is a converging lens?
5. List **three** parts of a camera.
6. HT What is the refractive index of a material?

Key Words Real image • Virtual image

Sound

When an object **vibrates** it produces sound.

The more rapid the vibrations, the higher the **frequency** of the sound. A higher frequency results in a sound with a higher **pitch**.

The larger the **amplitude** of the vibrations, the **louder** the sound will be.

The volume of a sound is also dependent on...
- the sensitivity of the ear
- the frequency of the sound.

The human ear is most sensitive to sounds around 2000Hz (2kHz). Some sounds are so high or so low pitched that you can't detect them at all.

The **decibel scale** is used to describe sound **intensity**. It isn't a linear scale. Increasing a sound by 10 decibels (dB) doubles its loudness.

Prolonged exposure to loud sounds can cause...
- permanent hearing loss
- tinnitus (persistent ringing in the ears).

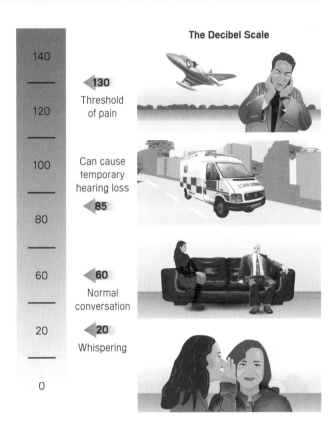

The Decibel Scale

140
120
100
80
60
20
0

130 Threshold of pain

Can cause temporary hearing loss 85

60 Normal conversation

20 Whispering

Sound Systems

You can make a simple sound system using a microphone, amplifier and loudspeaker.

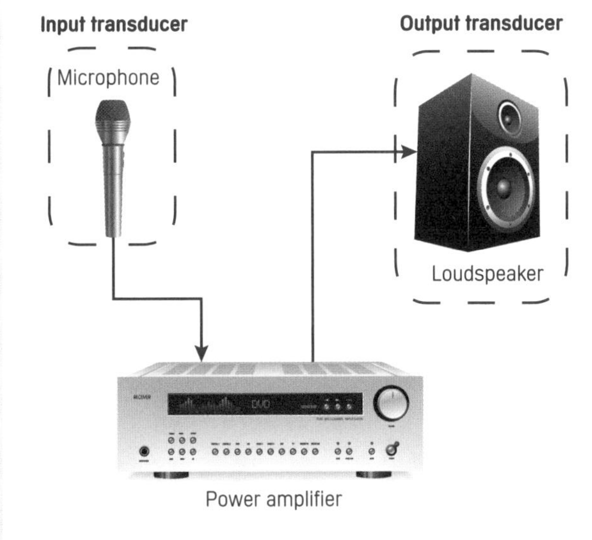

B2 Stage and Screen

Howl

Howl or **feedback** occurs when the sound from the speakers enters the microphone and is re-amplified and sent through the speakers again.

This loop will continue until the equipment is moved. The sound (howl/feedback) occurs at a single frequency. It can be avoided by...

- positioning the speakers in front of the microphone
- pointing the speakers away from the microphone
- placing the microphone close to the performer.

A Sound System that will Produce Howl

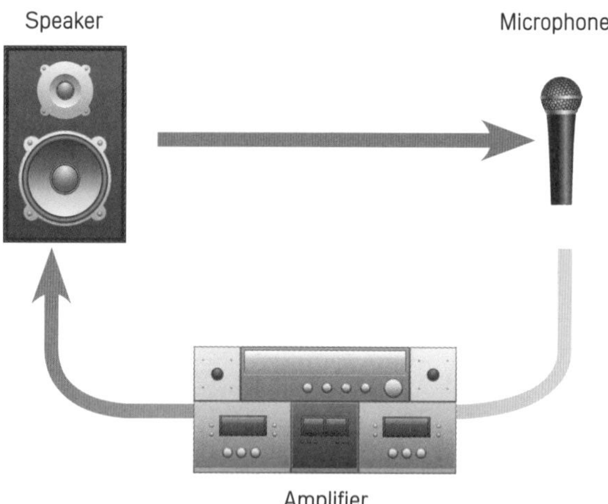

Absorbing and Reflecting Sound

Sound in a building is either **absorbed** or **reflected**:

- Hard, smooth, rigid materials, such as the glass in double glazing, are good at reflecting sound.
- Porous materials, such as carpet underlay and acoustic ceiling tiles, reduce sound intensity by absorbing it.

Venue acoustics are controlled using appropriate reflective and absorbing surfaces.

Reflective surfaces are placed and angled to produce good coverage of sound for the audience.

The seating area in the auditorium absorbs some sound. Additional absorbing surfaces include fabric-covered panels which absorb sound reflections.

Double glazing...

- reflects sound that could enter a venue
- reflects sound that could leave the venue.

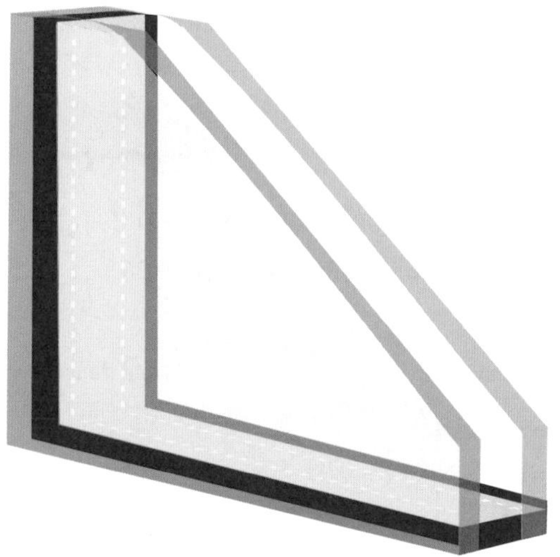

Quick Test

1. What frequency is the human ear most sensitive to?
2. Do loud sounds have a high frequency or a large amplitude?
3. Give **one** way in which howl can be prevented.
4. Why do concert venues have double glazed windows?

Reducing Damage Caused by Sound

Rigid structures can be damaged by vibrations. Methods used to prevent such damage isolate vibrations so that they are not carried by rigid structures. For example,...

- using **structures**, such as supporting floors with fluid-filled dampers and mounting systems in wire suspensions
- using **materials**, such as mounting the equipment on rubber pads.

HT Large buildings have a **low resonant frequency**. This makes them particularly susceptible to low frequency vibrations.

A low frequency sound can set up resonance in the building, causing the vibrations to get larger and larger until the structure collapses.

Indoor Performance Venues

Performance venue design requires control systems and health and safety features.

Lighting Circuits

A **switch** lets a current through only when it's pushed or pressed.

A **series circuit** with a switch:

- Both bulbs have to work for the circuit to be completed.
- The more bulbs in the circuit, the dimmer they become.

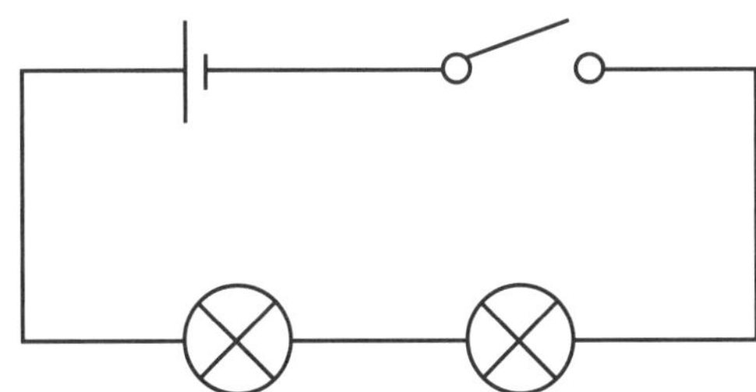

A **parallel circuit** with a single switch:

- Both bulbs are turned on/off by the switch.
- If one bulb burns out, the other stays lit.
- The bulbs are not dimmed when additional ones are added.

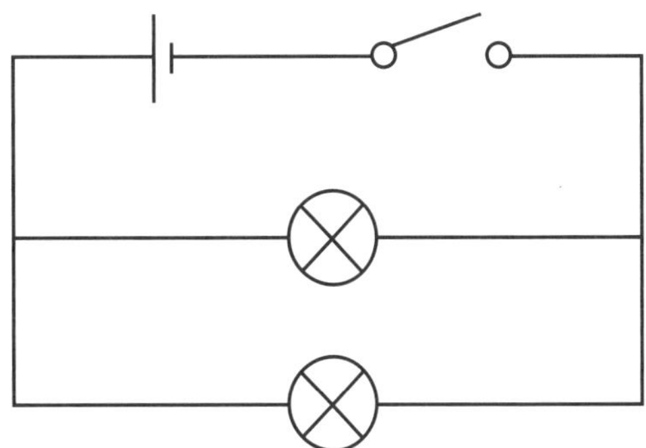

Lighting circuits are connected in parallel.

Lighting Control

The positioning of switches allows lights to be turned on or off in many combinations.

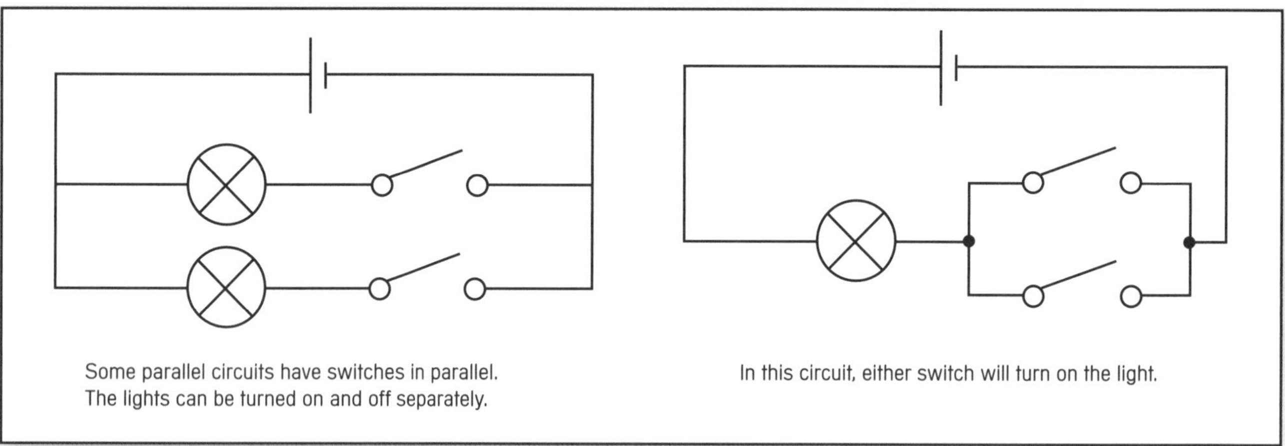

Some parallel circuits have switches in parallel. The lights can be turned on and off separately.

In this circuit, either switch will turn on the light.

Dimmers are used to adjust the brightness of a light. You can use a variable resistor as a dimmer. When the slider or control knob is moved, its **resistance** changes. When the resistance is increased, less current can get through.

Stage Lighting Dimmers

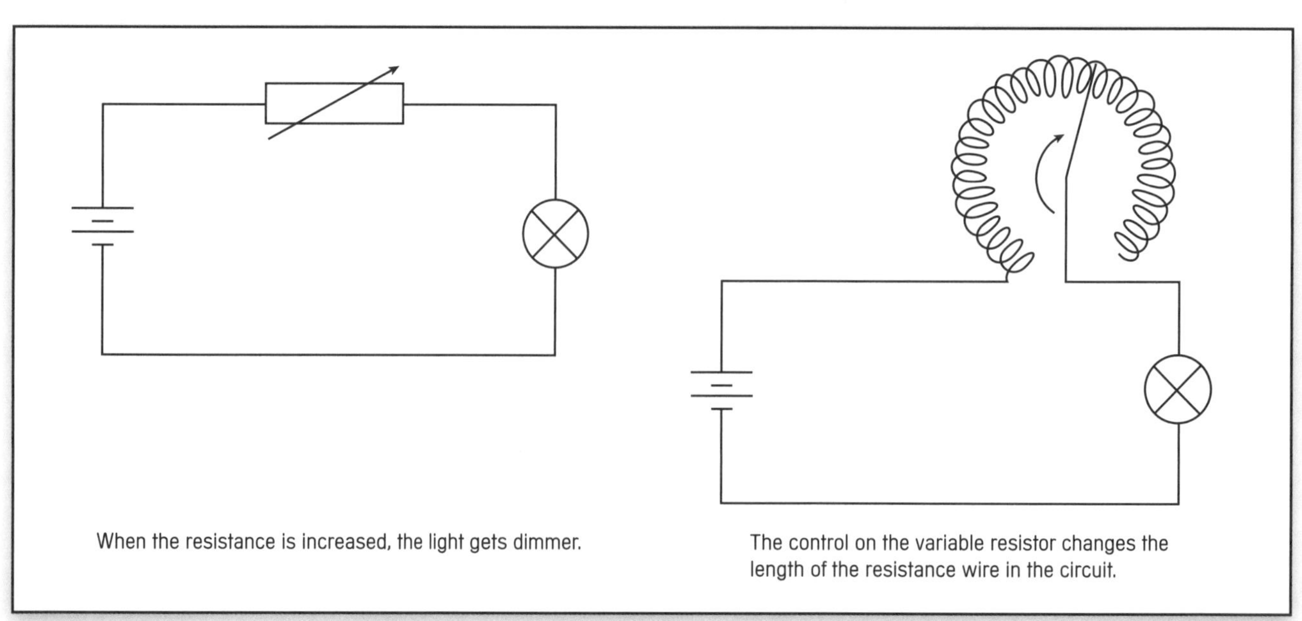

When the resistance is increased, the light gets dimmer.

The control on the variable resistor changes the length of the resistance wire in the circuit.

Key Words Dimmer • Resistance

Sources of Heat

Temperature control is a problem in crowded indoor performance venues. Sources of heat include...

- lighting
- large audiences.

Temperature control is helped by ventilation. Many modern venues use **natural ventilation**.

Lighting systems spread within the venue at different levels help to control heat.

Health and Safety Features

Health and safety features of indoor performance venues include...

- emergency lighting, for if the power fails
- emergency exits with clear signage
- fireproof safety curtain in theatres
- fire doors to contain the fire.

Venues plan and practise people flow in an evacuation and measure the evacuation time.

Quick Test

1. Give **one** advantage of using a parallel circuit instead of a series circuit in a lighting circuit.
2. What electrical component could be used to dim a light?
3. Give **two** sources of heat in an indoor performance venue.
4. List **three** safety features used in a theatre.

B2 Exam Practice Questions

1. Name **three** types of light source used in stage and screen. **[3]**

....

....

....

2. Complete the sentences below. **[3]**

Light sources such as .... lamps produce unwanted infrared radiation, which causes ....

Ultraviolet radiation is emitted by some light sources. It can cause ....

3. For a white light source, complete the table below. **[3]**

Colour of Filter	Colour of Light Absorbed	Colour of Light that Appears
Blue	....	....
....	Blue and green	....
....	....	Cyan

4. Label the parts of the camera in the diagram. **[4]**

1. ....
2. ....
3. ....
4. ....
5. ....

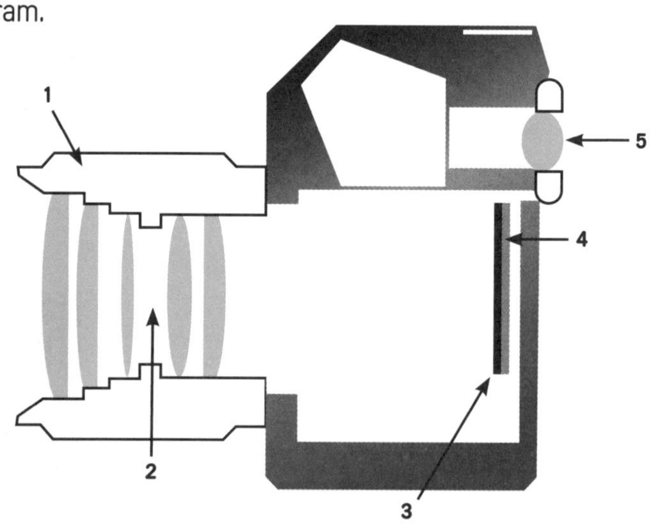

5. Complete the sentences below. **[4]**

Sounds with higher frequencies have a higher .... than sounds with lower frequencies.

The decibel scale is used to describe .... It is not a .... scale.

A sound of over .... dB would cause temporary hearing loss.

6 Draw straight lines to join the terms used to describe optical property with the correct definitions. **[4]**

Term	Definition
Reflective	A material that lets light pass through virtually unchanged
Refractive	A surface that light bounces off
Translucent	A material that allows light to pass through but scatters it
Transparent	A material that light can't pass through
Opaque	A material that can change the direction of light passing through it

7 The flow chart shows a simple sound system.

A → B → C

(a) Put the correct letter next to each component of the system. **[2]**

Amplifier .... Loudspeaker .... Microphone ....

(b) How are the components arranged to avoid howl? **[3]**

....

....

....

HT 8 Claire uses a camera to take a photograph of her friend Jodie, standing a long distance away. Jodie then moves close to the camera.

Explain how an image is formed on the image sensor of the camera, what happens to the image as Jodie moves closer, and how Claire can keep the image of Jodie in focus after she has moved closer to the camera.

The quality of written communication will be assessed in your answer to this question. **[6]**

....

....

....

....

....

....

....

Food Industries

Farming and biotechnology is used to produce the food we eat. Important parts of the UK food industry include ...

- wheat production for bread making
- barley production for beer
- cattle for milk
- biotechnology for beer and cheese.

A **chain** can be used to show every stage of **food production**. For example, the chain below shows the stages involved in the production of flour **from wheat**.

Growing
Wheat grown and **harvested**.

Transporting
Grains transported from farm to factory.

Processing
Wheat grains milled and processed into flour.

Storing
Flour bagged and stored in warehouse.

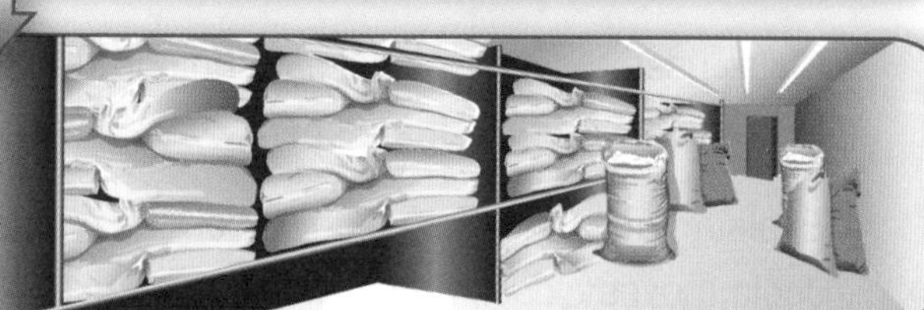

Delivering
Bags of flour delivered to supermarket and sold to homes.

Key Words Chain of food production • Harvest

People in the Food Industries

Large numbers of people in the UK work in the food industry. These include the following:

Food technologists who...
- study the biological, chemical and microbiological content of food
- design processes and machinery to ensure the consistency of the quality of food products, including their flavour, colour and texture
- develop manufacturing processes and recipes for new food and drink products.

Environmental health officers who...
- ensure the food we eat is of good quality and safe to eat
- carry out routine or unplanned visits to organisations working with food
- investigate complaints from the public
- investigate outbreaks of disease related to food.

Factory inspectors, who work in factories involved in food production, who...
- evaluate processes used in food manufacture, including quality, labelling and presentation
- design and carry out inspection programmes to assess the effectiveness of systems to ensure food quality
- sample food products
- ensure that standards of food legislation are applied, and use criminal procedures if they are not, where appropriate
- follow up complaints.

Testing Quality and Safety

Environmental health officers, factory inspectors and food technologists who monitor the food chain are called **enforcement officers**.

Food and food products are tested during development in order to...
- prevent poor quality
- identify and correct issues
- prevent the sale of a contaminated product.

Testing for quality and safety can take place at different stages in the production cycle.

Regulating the Food Industry

The purpose of organisations that **regulate** agriculture and food production is to...
- protect the health and safety of the public, and people involved in the food industry
- ensure the welfare of animals
- protect the environment.

Quick Test

1. List **three** stages in the food production chain.
2. Write down **three** types of practitioner in the food industry.
3. Write down **two** reasons for testing food products during development.

Key Words Food technologist • Environmental health officer • Factory inspector

Wheat Production

The people involved in wheat production include…
- crop breeders
- farmers
- chemical (**fertilisers** and pesticides) manufacturers.

Their aim is to produce good quality bread-making flour at competitive prices.

Crop scientists investigate the performance of wheat varieties. They can do this by measuring…
- **germination rates**: the number of seeds that germinate ÷ the number of seeds sown
- **dry mass**: the mass of the crop, dried until the mass is constant.

Stages of Wheat Production

1 Soil preparation

HT – The soil is prepared by ploughing.
– The remains of the previous year's crop are ploughed into the soil.

2 Sowing the seeds

HT – Sowing the seeds is called **drilling**.
– A channel is produced in the ground that the seeds fall into.

3 The use of chemicals

HT – Fertilisers, herbicides, fungicides and insecticides may be applied to increase yields.

4 Harvesting

HT – The crop is harvested using a combine harvester.
– The grain is separated from the straw.
– The straw can be collected in bales and used as animal food.

5 Drying and storage

HT – The grain is dried and stored in buildings.

Key Words Fertiliser • Drilling

Conditions for Wheat Production

Wheat grows best on loam soils that are medium in texture and have organic matter. Its growth requires...

- **water** – wheat needs 25 to 60cm of water per year. In the UK, it gets this from the rain.
- **nutrients** – farmers add to the nutrients in the soil with **fertilisers**.
- **pH** – the optimum pH range is 6 to 8. Wheat doesn't grow well in acid soils.

Crop Varieties

Several species of wheat are grown, including bread wheat for bread, and durum wheat for pasta. Durum wheats have a higher protein content.

The features of the commercial **crop varieties of wheat**:

- Selected to have appropriate growing periods to produce **maximum yields** according to the climate.
- **Winter wheats** are sown in the autumn and harvested the following August; Spring wheats are sown in the spring, avoiding hard winters.
- Good **nutritional quality**: the grain is high in protein and starch.
- Produce flour with a good texture.
- Good **resistance to disease**.
- Short sturdy stems that don't fall over easily in the wind.

Getting the Best Yield

Using chemicals increases crop **yields** but there are also risks associated with their use.

Chemical	Risks from Using Chemical
Insecticides • Prevent damage to the wheat by insect pests	• Toxic to humans and other organisms • Become concentrated along food chains • Residues can be left on foods
Fungicides • Prevent the growth of fungi on the wheat and the diseases the fungi produce	• Can be toxic
Herbicides • Slow the growth of weeds, which would otherwise compete for light, water and nutrients	• Many are harmful to humans • Residues can be left on foods
Fertilisers • Release nutrients quickly into the soil for uptake by plants • Increase growth and yield of the crop	• Can be washed into surrounding streams/rivers (they become enriched with nutrients – **eutrophication**) • The increased growth of algae deprives the water of oxygen and organisms die.

Key Words Fertiliser • pH • Yield • Insecticide • Fungicide • Herbicide

B3 Agriculture, Biotechnology and Food

Inorganic (Intensive) and Organic Methods of Farming Wheat

Inorganic (Intensive) Methods	Organic Methods
• Use insecticides, fungicides and herbicides to get maximum growth	• Use natural pesticides that cause minimum harm to the environment. • Natural predators of insect pests are encouraged. • Weeds are removed by mechanical methods such as hoeing.
• Use inorganic fertilisers to get maximum yields	• Use organic fertilisers such as manure, used hops and seaweed.
• Varieties selected to give maximum yields.	• Wheat varieties selected to grow well in organic conditions.

HT The Costs of Wheat Production

The factors that affect the costs of wheat production are...

- soil preparation
- spraying
- application of fertilisers
- harvesting
- poor weather reducing yields; optimum weather increasing yields.

The Dairy Industry

Dairy cattle are reared to produce large volumes of milk. Products made from milk include...

- cream
- butter
- cheese
- cottage cheese
- yoghurt.

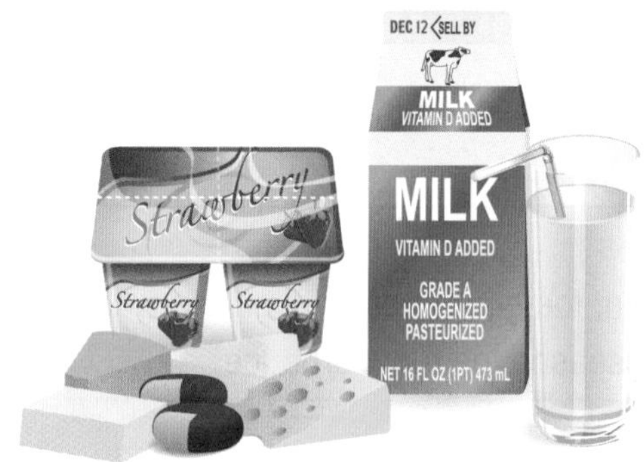

Factors Affecting Milk Quality and Yield

The **breed** of cow and the **animal husbandry** affect milk quality and milk yield.

Cattle breeds that are used in milk production...

- are bred to produce large volumes of milk
- can live for a long time and therefore produce milk over a number of years
- can produce high quality milk even when kept on poor pasture land
- are less muscular than cattle bred for meat, and often small so that less space is needed to keep them
- are bred to be resistant to disease.

Key Words Breed • Animal husbandry

Processing Milk

Most milk used to produce milk products is first **pasteurised**. It's heat treated (it's heated to around 70°C for a short period of time) and cooled rapidly to kill harmful microorganisms (**pathogens**).

UHT milk is heated to an ultra-high temperature (at least 135°C) to kill all the microorganisms in the milk.

Milk contains around 3.5% fat. Skimmed milk is made by separating off the fat. It contains 0.1–0.3% fat.

Testing Milk Freshness

A quick test used to find the freshness of milk is the **resazurin** test.

Resazurin (which is blue in colour) is added to the milk. The milk is incubated for 30 minutes at 35°C.

According to the freshness of the milk, the resazurin will turn a purple or pink colour, or go colourless if it contains a large number of bacteria.

HT The respiration of bacteria in the milk causes the resazurin to change colour.

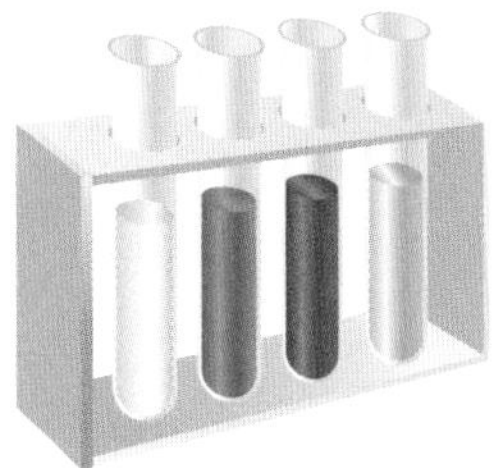

Animal Husbandry

Animal husbandry is how the animal is cared for. Good husbandry is important for the health and well-being of the cow, so it's also important in milk production.

Good animal husbandry involves…

- good nutrition (appropriate food and water)
- good hygiene and health
- preventing and controlling disease
- a good living environment (including temperature and shelter).

Artificial Insemination

Farm animals can be artificially inseminated.

Artificial insemination involves four stages:

1. Selection of animals – the parents are selected to meet particular characteristics.
2. Collection of sperm – methods include the following:
   - Arousing the male with a 'teaser' female or a decoy animal. As the male tries to mount the female, breeders direct its penis into a collection reservoir.
   - Electroejaculation, where mild electrical stimulation is applied to the accessory sex glands. This is useful when a female, or decoy, isn't available.
3. Storage of sperm – a straw containing the sperm is dipped into liquid nitrogen so that it rapidly freezes. The 'sperm straw' can be stored until it's required.
4. Timing of sperm insertion – the sperm is inserted into the female when she is most fertile. Half of the semen is injected into each side of the uterus using an insemination pipette and a laparoscope.

Key Words Pasteurisation • UHT • Resazurin • Artificial insemination

B3 Agriculture, Biotechnology and Food

Selective Breeding

Mating only the animals with particular characteristics required is known as **selective breeding**. Animals with poor qualities aren't allowed to breed.

Selective breeding can improve productivity because the offspring should inherit the desirable traits from its parents.

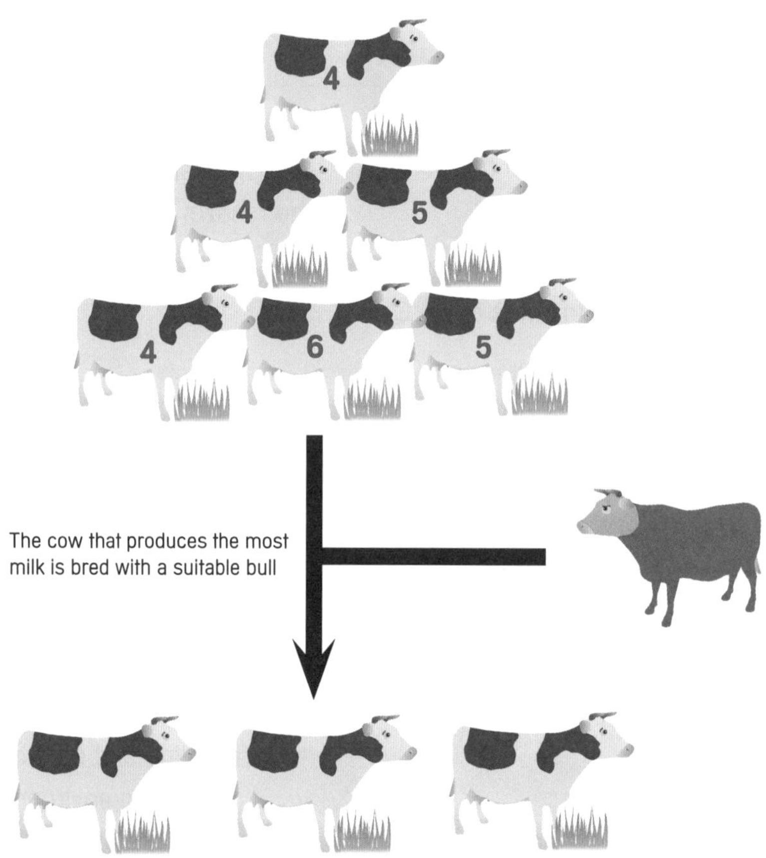
4
4
5
4
6
5
The cow that produces the most milk is bred with a suitable bull

From the offspring, those that produce the most milk are bred on

HT Controlling the Timing of Fertilisation

The timing of fertilisation can sometimes be controlled accurately by giving **hormones** to the female to ensure that an egg is fertilised.

Quick Test

1. State **two** factors that influence the quality of milk produced by cattle.
2. What does the term 'animal husbandry' mean?
3. Give **three** examples of good animal husbandry.
4. Write down **two** techniques used to treat milk.

Key Words Selective breeding • Hormone

Biotechnology and Food

Biotechnology is the use of biological systems or living organisms for a specific purpose.

People in the biotechnology industries include...
- microbiologists
- biochemists
- genetic engineers
- engineers
- quality control managers.

Microorganisms – which include **yeasts**, **bacteria** and **viruses** – are commonly used to produce food and drink:
- **Yeast** is used in the production of alcohol for drinks or fuel, and bread.
- **Bacteria** are used to turn milk into yoghurt and cheese.
- A **fungus** is used to turn flour waste into mycoprotein.
- Microorganisms can provide **enzymes** such as chymosin, which is used in the production of cheese.

Some microorganisms can spoil products by...
- feeding on them
- contaminating them with their waste products.

There are also some microorganisms that cause **disease** and **infection**.

These are called **pathogens**.

For these reasons, microbiologists take precautionary measures, known as **aseptic techniques**.

Aseptic techniques ensure sterile conditions. They prevent contamination of the food, and contamination of the environment by killing any unwanted microorganisms. This is achieved by...
- thoroughly cleaning and heat-treating equipment
- wearing protective hats
- regular hand washing.

Samples are taken regularly to check whether unwanted microorganisms are present.

Aseptic Technique

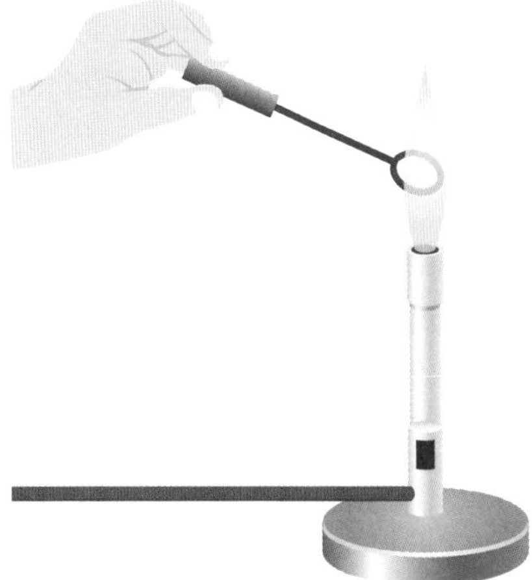

Quick Test

1. Name **three** types of microorganism.
2. What technique is used to prevent contamination when working with microorganisms?
3. How do microorganisms spoil food?
4. What are microorganisms that cause disease called?

Key Words Biotechnology • Microorganism • Enzyme • Pathogen • Aseptic technique

B3 Agriculture, Biotechnology and Food

Respiration

Energy can be released from food in two ways…
- **aerobic respiration**
- **anaerobic respiration**.

Aerobic respiration breaks down glucose molecules by combining them with oxygen. The majority of organisms respire aerobically. Aerobic respiration is also the main method of releasing energy from food.

The word equation for aerobic respiration is:

Glucose + Oxygen → Carbon dioxide + Water (+ Energy)

Anaerobic respiration takes place in the absence of oxygen. It's less efficient than aerobic respiration and produces less energy.

The word equation for anaerobic respiration in yeast is:

Glucose → Carbon dioxide + Alcohol (+ Energy)

Bacteria called Lactobacilli (for example, *Lactobacillus bulgaricus*) are used when making many milk products.

The word equation for anaerobic respiration in Lactobacilli is:

HT You need to know the symbol equation for the following reactions.

The **aerobic** respiration of yeast:

Glucose + Oxygen → Carbon dioxide + Water (+ Energy)
$C_6H_{12}O_6 + 6O_2 \longrightarrow 6CO_2 + H_2O$

The **anaerobic** respiration of yeast:

Glucose → Carbon dioxide + Ethanol (+ Energy)
$C_6H_{12}O_6 \longrightarrow 2CO_2 + 2C_2H_5OH$

The **anaerobic** respiration of Lactobacilli:

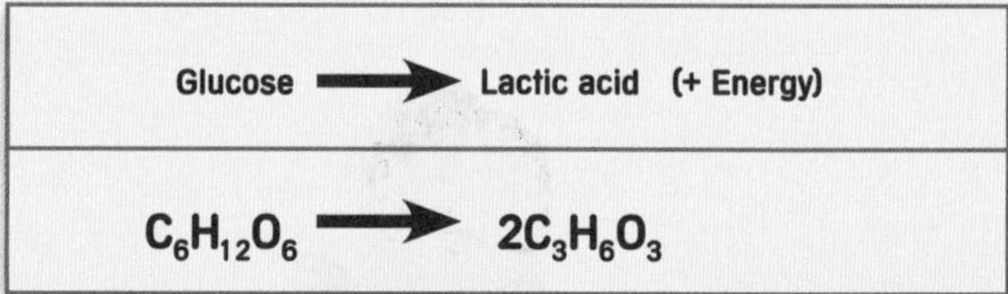

Fermentation

Microorganisms are used to produce food products by a process called **fermentation**.

Yeast can change its respiration from aerobic to anaerobic when the oxygen runs out. Yeast fermentation has aerobic and anaerobic stages. Yeast is used to make bread and alcohol for fuel and drinks.

Yoghurt is made by the anaerobic fermentation of the sugar lactose to produce lactic acid.

Other important fermentations include…
- coffee – coffee beans are fermented to remove the slimy layer that covers the bean.
- soya sauce – made by using a fungus to ferment soya beans.

Products are sometimes **processed** after fermentation is complete. For example…
- yeast extract, e.g. Marmite is made by processing yeast cells after a beer fermentation
- mycoprotein, produced by fermenting flour waste using the fungus *Fusarium*, is processed to lower its nutritional content.

Key Words Aerobic respiration • Anaerobic respiration • Fermentation

Culturing Microorganisms

The main stages of population growth of a culture of microorganisms are:

1. **The lag phase** – growth is slow as the microorganisms adapt to the new living conditions.
2. **The log phase (exponential growth)** – the microorganisms double in number every few minutes.
3. **The stationary phase** – the increasing population of microorganisms competes for a reducing quantity of nutrients.
4. **The death phase (senescence)** – toxins produced by the microorganisms build up to a high level and, combined with the lack of nutrients, the population dies.

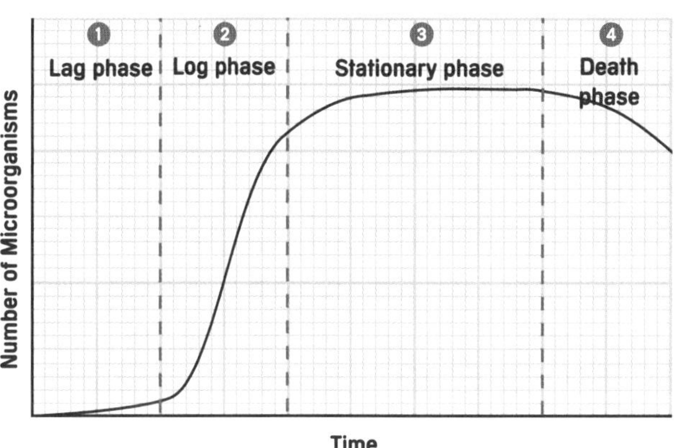

HT You may be required to interpret data on the population growth of microorganisms.

Batch and Continuous Cultures

A **batch culture** is a **closed system culture**. The microorganisms grow in a large container such as a vat.

When the product has been produced, it's removed from the vat. The vat is then cleaned and the process started again.

A **continuous culture** is where microorganisms are grown in a system where the culture medium is **continuously replenished with fresh nutrients**. The product is removed continuously.

Environmental conditions can be kept constant and wastes produced by the microorganisms don't build up.

Advantages and Disadvantages of Batch and Continuous Cultures

	Batch Culture	Continuous Culture
Advantages	Easy to set up and maintain	Conditions remain ideal so microorganisms can be grown over a long period of time
Disadvantages	Conditions will quickly change from ideal due to the growth of the microorganisms	Expensive to set up and maintain (needs computers to monitor)

Quick Test

1. Name the **four** phases in the growth of a population of microorganisms.
2. Write a word equation for the anaerobic respiration of yeast.
3. Give the advantage of using continuous culture to produce a food product.

Key Words Batch culture • Continuous culture

B3 Agriculture, Biotechnology and Food

Genetic Modification

Genetically modified (**GM**) microorganisms are used to produce both food ingredients and enzymes used in food processing.

A **gene** controls the production of a protein. In **genetic modification**, a gene that causes the production of a desirable **protein** in one organism is introduced into another organism. The GM organism can then produce the protein that the original organism produced.

For example, cheese depends on the curdling (or **coagulation**) of milk. Old methods used rennet from calves' stomachs. GM bacteria are now often used to make the active ingredient of rennet (an enzyme called chymosin).

Other products made using genetically modified microorganisms include yoghurt and food additives such as vitamins and flavourings.

HT **DNA** is the genetic material of all organisms. It forms all the **genes** that 'code' for all the particular proteins that an organism needs.

In genetic modification...

- the gene that produces a particular protein is cut out of one organism's DNA
- the gene is then inserted into the DNA of another organism (using a carrier such as a plasmid)
- the beneficiary organism can then produce the protein itself
- identical genetic copies of the modified organism are made by **cloning**.

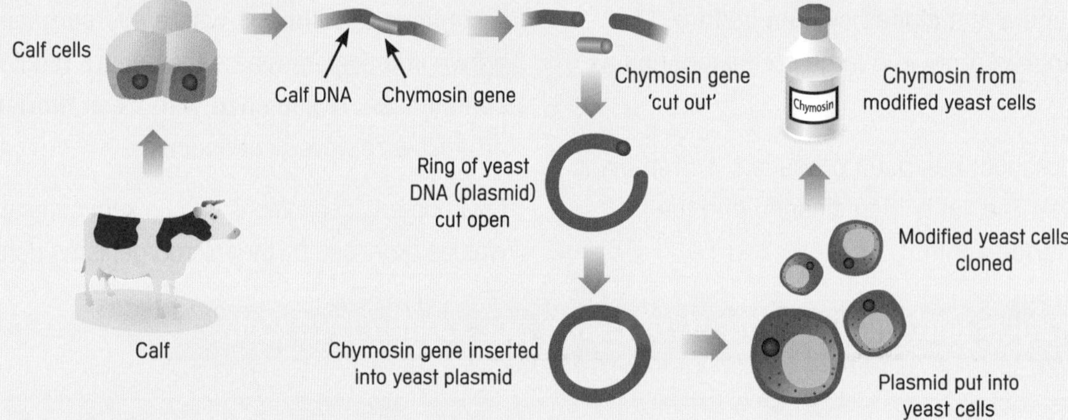

Fermenters

A **fermenter** or **bioreactor** is a controlled environment that provides ideal conditions for microorganisms to live in. Fermenters are used to produce large quantities of microorganisms or their products, e.g. alcohol. An industrial fermenter or bioreactor has several components:

- **Stirrer** – keeps the microorganisms in suspension; keeps the contents (e.g. food, oxygen) distributed evenly and maintains an even temperature.
- **Outlet tap** – opens to collect the product.
- **Sterile air supply** – provides oxygen for respiration (if oxygen is required). Air is sterilised in order to prevent contamination.
- **Water-cooled jacket** – removes heat produced by the respiring microorganisms.
- Sensors and datalogging software:
  - **pH sensor** – monitors the pH of the mixture.
  - **Temperature sensor** – monitors the temperature of the mixture.

Key Words Gene • Genetic modification • Cloning • Fermenter • Bioreactor

Fermenters (Cont.)

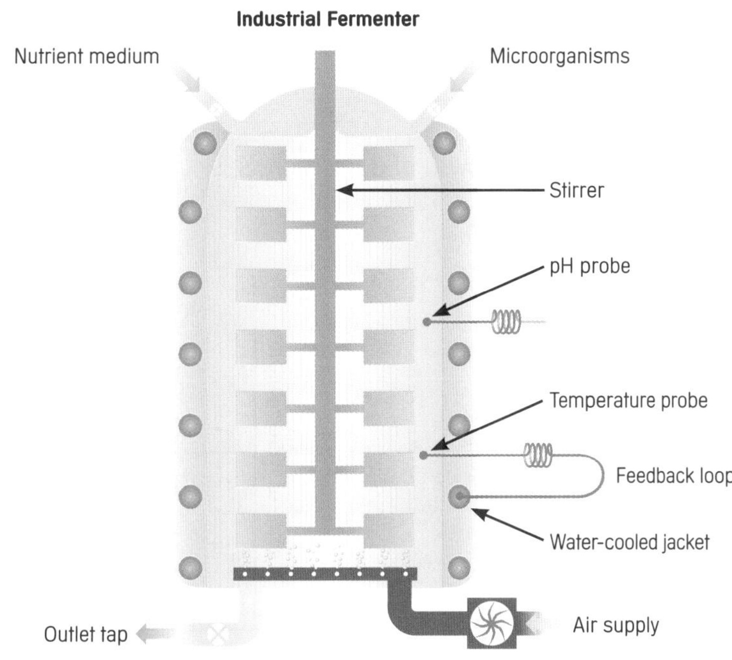

HT Monitoring and Control of Bioreactors

Conditions in a bioreactor are monitored and controlled automatically. For example, in the fermenter on this page, temperature is controlled by a feedback loop:

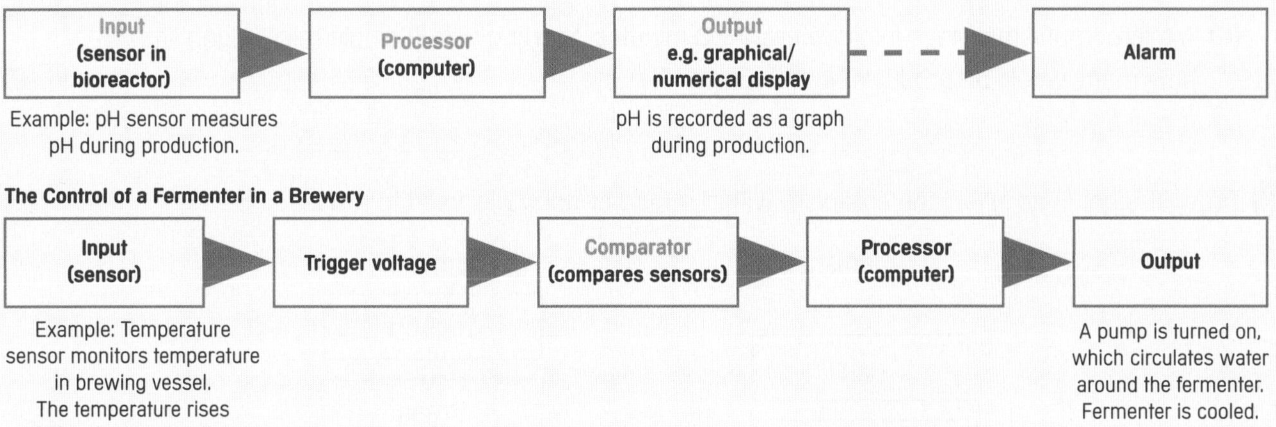

Quick Test

1. What is meant by genetic modification?
2. How is genetic modification used in modern cheese production?
3. Why is a stirrer used in a bioreactor?
4. What is the name of the devices used to monitor temperature and pH in a bioreactor?

Key Words Input • Processor • Output • Comparator

B3 Exam Practice Questions

1. Give **three** reasons why organisations that regulate the food industry exist. **[3]**

   1. ....

   2. ....

   3. ....

2. The graph shows the stages in the growth of a microorganism.

   (a) Write the labels for the stages **A–D**. **[4]**

   A ....

   B ....

   C ....

   D ....

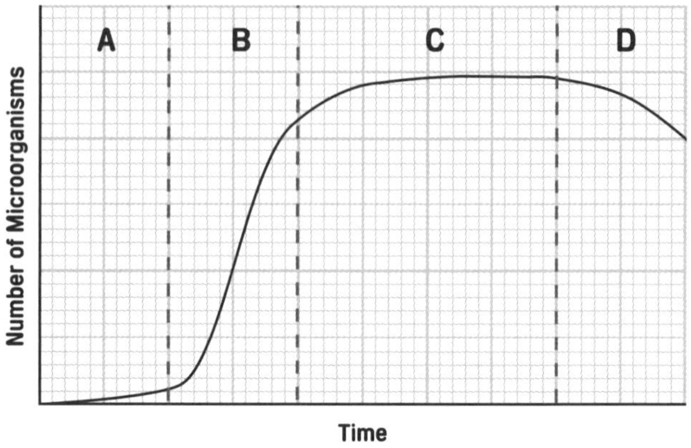

   (b) At what stage is the microorganism adapting to its environment? **[1]**

   ....

   (c) At what stage is the microorganism growing and reproducing most rapidly? **[1]**

   ....

   (d) A microorganism divides into two every 20 minutes. Starting with a single microorganism, how many would be produced in 2 hours? **[2]**

   ....

3. Draw straight lines to join the organism with the food or drink it is used to produce. **[2]**

Organism	Food/drink
Yeast	Yoghurt
Bacteria	Bread
	Alcohol

4. **(a)** Write out the word equation for the aerobic respiration of yeast. **[2]**

   ....

   (b) Write out the word equation for the anaerobic respiration of Lactobacilli. **[2]**

   ....

5 Batch and continuous cultures are methods for growing microorganisms.
Describe the advantages and disadvantages of the two different methods. **[4]**

6 Explain the benefits and risks of using chemical (inorganic) fertilisers on a wheat crop.
The quality of written communication will be assessed in your answer to this question. **[6]**

HT 7 **(a)** Label the flow chart below to show how pH is monitored in a bioreactor.
If the pH rises, an alarm is set off. **[4]**

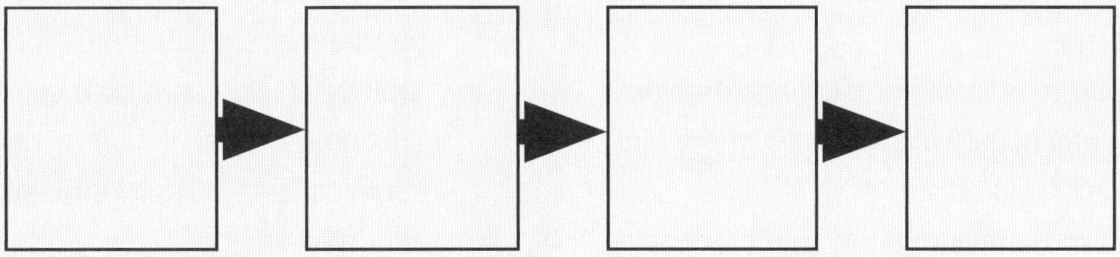

(b) When the temperature in a bioreactor falls too low, a heater is switched on.
Label the flow chart below to show how this is done. **[5]**

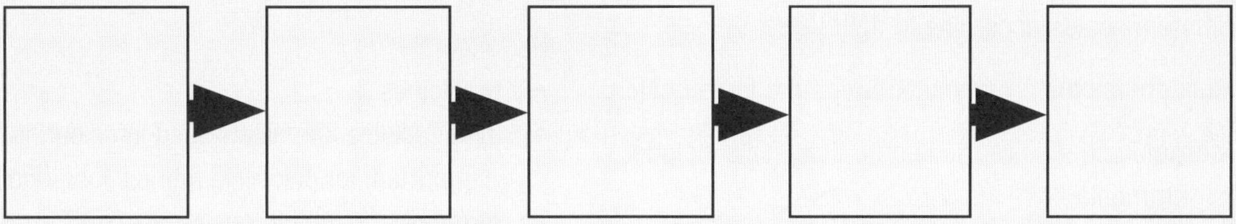

B4 Making Chemical Products

The Chemical and Pharmaceutical Industries

Everything is made of chemicals. Some chemicals occur in nature and, from these, many others are manufactured.

The chemical industry is one of the most important in the UK. It employs a wide range of people from research chemists through to marketing and finance specialists.

People and Organisations

Technicians carry out routine procedures in chemical laboratories that it would not be appropriate for scientists to spend time doing. They also support the scientists in other ways. The roles of technicians include...

- sampling procedures
- testing and analysing samples
- using equipment and chemicals in these procedures
- maintaining equipment in the laboratories
- ensuring that chemicals are stored safely
- making up product formulations.

HT The Grades of Chemicals Used in Chemical Laboratories

Depending on the work they're doing, scientists in the chemical industry use chemicals of different purity or **grade**.

- **Technical** – the least pure, cheapest grade. Used in preliminary experiments where high purity isn't required.
- **Laboratory** – medium purity and cost, for everyday use in the laboratory. Used for manufacturing many products, but unsuitable for pharmaceutical or food formulations.
- **Analytical** – purest and most expensive grade. This grade is needed when carrying out a chemical analysis, or formulating food products and medicines.

The Scale of Chemical Production

The chemical industry produces chemicals on different scales according to their value.

Bulk chemicals are manufactured on a large scale.

Inorganic chemicals made on a bulk scale include...

- ammonia
- sulfuric acid
- sodium hydroxide.

Fine chemicals are made on a small scale.

For example...

- medicines
- **dyes** (soluble chemicals used in colouring) – important for colouring fabrics, food and in inks
- **pigments** (insoluble chemicals used in colouring) – important for paints, inks, plastics, cosmetics and food.

Key Words Bulk chemical • Fine chemical • Dye • Pigment

The Scale of Chemical Production (Cont.)

Metals such as iron and copper are extracted from their ores on a large scale.

The main uses of copper are...

- in the transmission of electricity – as electrical wiring and electrical contacts
- in plumbing and construction.

The main uses of iron are...

- to produce steel, which is used in construction (buildings, bridges), machines, tools, motor vehicles, ships, cutlery and surgical instruments
- nutritional supplements.

HT New Chemical Products

New chemical products, such as new medical drugs, are the result of research and development, and testing.

Steps in the development of a new drug include the following:

- **Discovery**: A potential drug could be discovered from a natural source or by accident, or research scientists may be looking at a particular type of chemical.
- **Research** its chemical properties and structure: can it be extracted easily, and is it stable, or does it break down quickly?
- **Testing**: Is it effective, is it toxic, and/or does it have side effects? The chemical is first tested in the laboratory, then on animals and finally on humans (clinical trials).
- **Approval**.

If suitable, new chemicals produced in the laboratory must then be produced on an industrial scale. This is called **scaling up**.

Chemical procedures can occur differently when transferred to a large scale. The issues that have to be dealt with include...

- the type of reaction vessel may have to be changed or modified
- the method used to transfer liquids from one stage in the production to another
- how the chemicals are mixed
- how mixtures of chemicals are heated and cooled
- how the product is separated from the reaction mixture
- how the product is purified.

Quick Test

1. What is meant by a bulk chemical?
2. Give **one** example of a fine chemical.
3. Give **one** example of a use of...
   (a) copper
   (b) iron.
4. Name **three** grades of chemicals.

B4 Making Chemical Products

HT Chemical Production

Chemical production can be a **batch** or **continuous process**.

	Batch Process	Continuous Process
The process	Occurs in stages: • The chemical reactants are fed into the vessel • The reaction takes place • The products are removed.	All the steps are going on continuously – as the products are removed, more reactants are fed in.
Advantages	• Good for small-scale production of pharmaceuticals and other fine chemicals that don't have to be produced all the time. • Often low set-up costs. • Any contamination is confined to individual batches. • Often easier to scale up.	• Good for large-scale production of chemicals that must be produced continuously. • The product can be very pure. • Continuous operation can be very efficient – the reactors can be run in a steady state in which conditions are maintained.
Disadvantages	• Frequent shutdown means that it's labour and energy intensive. • The chemical product can vary from one batch to another.	• Usually high set-up costs • Maintenance will stop production. • Contaminations affect the whole production. • Not useful for small-scale production.

Health and Safety

Because chemicals carry potential dangers, governments impose **regulations** on the chemical industry. The regulations control...

- chemical processes
- the storage of chemicals
- the transportation of chemicals
- research and development of chemicals.

In the UK, the **Health and Safety Executive** (**HSE**) regulates the risks to health and safety arising from the extraction, manufacture and use of chemicals.

Hazardous chemicals are labelled with these standard **hazchem** symbols, as appropriate.

Before carrying out practical work, scientists identify hazards and risks and ways of managing these. They perform a **risk assessment**.

Explosive

Harmful

Irritant

Toxic

Corrosive

Oxidising

Highly Flammable

Key Words Batch process • Continuous process

Chemical Symbols

All the **elements** in the **periodic table** are represented by a different symbol.

You need to learn the symbols for the **chemical elements** shown opposite.

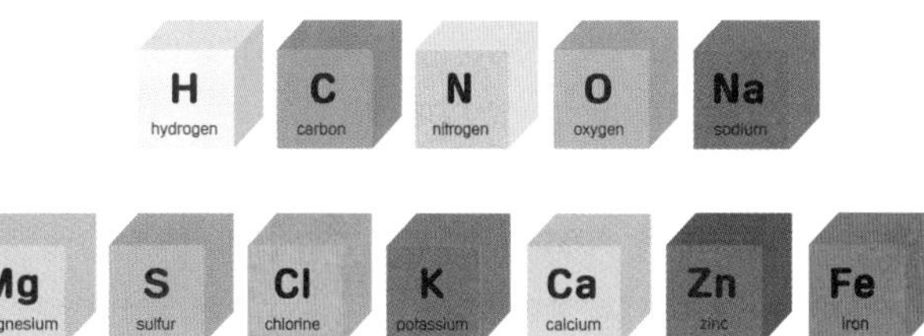

Chemical Formulae

When elements react they become joined together to form a **compound**. Chemical **formulae** are used to show…

- the different elements in a compound
- the number of atoms of each element in one molecule of the compound.

A small number that sits below the line multiplies only the symbol that comes immediately before it.

A number that's the same size as the letters multiplies all the symbols that come after it.

A bracket around two or more symbols means that all the atoms within the bracket are multiplied by the number outside the bracket.

For example, calcium nitrate has the chemical formula $Ca(NO_3)_2$.

The formula of calcium nitrate contains…

- one calcium atom
- two nitrogen atoms
- six oxygen atoms.

If you see $2Ca(NO_3)_2$ in a chemical equation, the '2' means that there are two molecules of calcium nitrate involved.

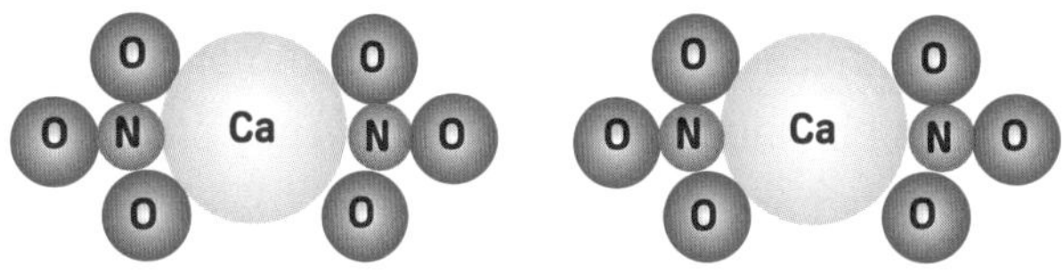

HT Chemical Formulae

You need to know the formulae for the following **oxides**, **hydroxides** and **salts** (chlorides, carbonates, sulfates and nitrates):

Chemical	Formula
Ammonia	NH_3
Copper(II) oxide	CuO
Magnesium oxide	MgO
Zinc oxide	ZnO
Magnesium hydroxide	$Mg(OH)_2$
Potassium hydroxide	KOH
Sodium hydroxide	NaOH

Chemical	Formula
Calcium carbonate	$CaCO_3$
Magnesium carbonate	$MgCO_3$
Zinc carbonate	$ZnCO_3$
Calcium chloride	$CaCl_2$
Potassium chloride	KCl
Sodium chloride	NaCl

Chemical	Formula
Potassium nitrate	KNO_3
Sodium nitrate	$NaNO_3$
Magnesium sulfate	$MgSO_4$
Sodium sulfate	Na_2SO_4
Zinc sulfate	$ZnSO_4$
Carbon dioxide	CO_2
Water	H_2O

Key Words Element • Compound • Formula

B4 Making Chemical Products

Representing Reactions

Word equations are used to represent chemical reactions. For example:

Carbon + Oxygen → Carbon dioxide

HT Balanced symbol equations can also be used to represent reactions. The equation for this reaction between carbon and oxygen is:

$$C(s) + O_2(g) \longrightarrow CO_2(g)$$

HT Relative Formula Mass

The **relative formula mass (M_r)** of a compound is the sum of the **relative atomic masses (A_r)** of each of its elements.

To calculate M_r you need to know...

- the formula of the compound
- the relative atomic mass (A_r) of each of the atoms involved (given in the periodic table).

Making Useful Chemicals

Useful chemicals can be obtained from natural materials obtained from the ground. They are...

- extracted or purified, or
- manufactured from these starting materials.

Ammonia is manufactured from nitrogen (extracted from the air) and hydrogen (manufactured from natural gas).

Sulfuric acid is manufactured from sulfur dioxide (produced by burning sulfur, or a sulfur-containing ore, in air), reacted with oxygen and water.

Sodium hydroxide is manufactured by the electrolysis of brine (salt water).

Neutralisation is a type of chemical reaction that happens when an acid and an alkali react. A main use of ammonia and sulfuric acid is to make **salts** such as fertilisers by neutralisation.

As well as fertilisers, salts are often ingredients of foods, medicines and other products.

Quick Test

1. What raw materials are used to produce...
   (a) ammonia?
   (b) sulfuric acid?
   (c) sodium hydroxide?

Key Words Relative formula mass (M_r) • Relative atomic mass (A_r)

Acids

The **pH scale** is used to measure of the acidity or alkalinity of an **aqueous solution**, across a 14-point scale.

Acids are substances that have a pH less than 7. You should know the chemical formula for the following common acids:

Acid	Formula
Hydrochloric acid	HCl
Sulfuric acid	H_2SO_4
Nitric acid	HNO_3

Below are some characteristic reactions of acids:

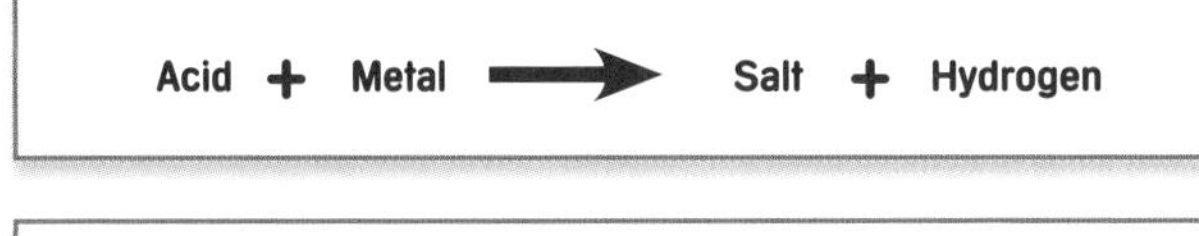

Acid + Metal oxide → Salt + Water

Acid + Metal carbonate → Salt + Water + Carbon dioxide

Alkalis

Alkalis dissolve in water to produce solutions that have a pH above 7.

Alkalis include oxides and hydroxides. They **neutralise** acids to form salts.

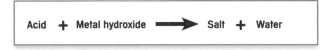

Neutralising Hydrochloric Acid with Potassium Hydroxide

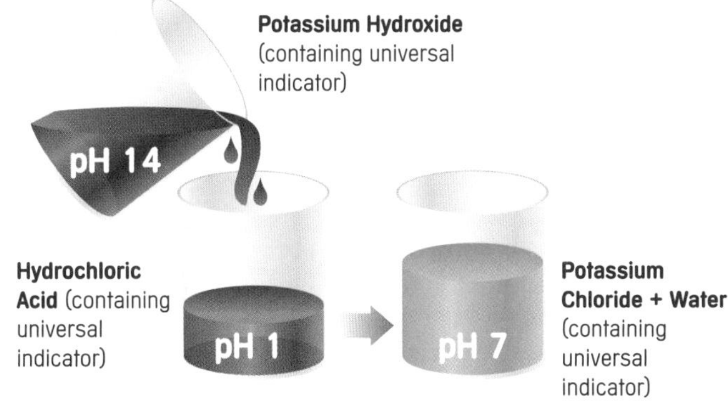

Preparation of Salts

You should be familiar with the terms used below.

A **soluble** chemical is a **solute** (solid) which will dissolve in a **solvent** (liquid) to make a **solution**.

An **insoluble** chemical will not dissolve in a solvent.

An **aqueous solution** is a solution made with water as the solvent.

A **non-aqueous solution** is made with any solvent other than water.

Precipitation is the formation of a **precipitate** (insoluble solid) when two solutions are mixed.

Filtration is the passing of a mixture through a porous material to separate solid particles from a liquid. The **filtrate** is the clear liquid that passes through the filter.

A **residue** is any matter left behind by a chemical **reaction**. An **insoluble residue** is any insoluble substance left behind after a **filtration** or other similar process.

Evaporation is the process of slowly heating a product to remove water.

Crystallisation is the formation of a solid during cooling of the product.

Key Words pH scale • Aqueous solution • Acid • Alkali • Soluble • Insoluble • Precipitation

Making Insoluble Salts

An **insoluble salt** is made by mixing together **two solutions** using the following method:

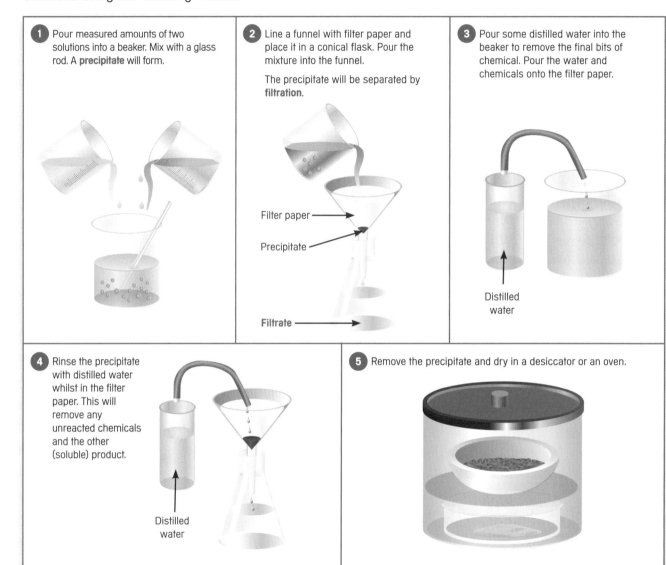

1. Pour measured amounts of two solutions into a beaker. Mix with a glass rod. A **precipitate** will form. 
2. Line a funnel with filter paper and place it in a conical flask. Pour the mixture into the funnel.

   The precipitate will be separated by **filtration**.

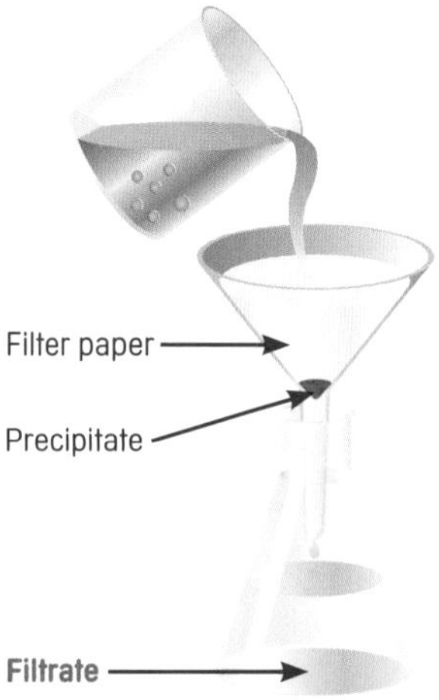

   Filter paper
   Precipitate
   Filtrate
3. Pour some distilled water into the beaker to remove the final bits of chemical. Pour the water and chemicals onto the filter paper.

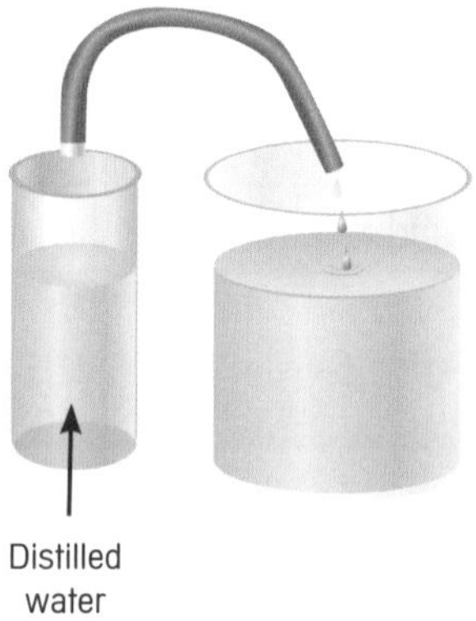

   Distilled water
4. Rinse the precipitate with distilled water whilst in the filter paper. This will remove any unreacted chemicals and the other (soluble) product.

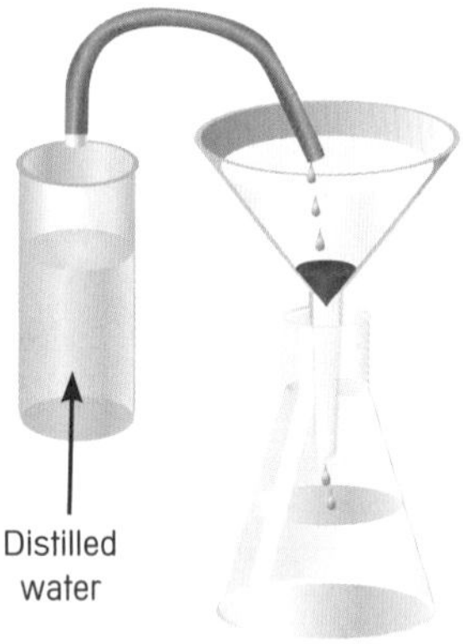

   Distilled water
5. Remove the precipitate and dry in a desiccator or an oven.

Examples of insoluble salts that can be made by reacting two solutions include the following:

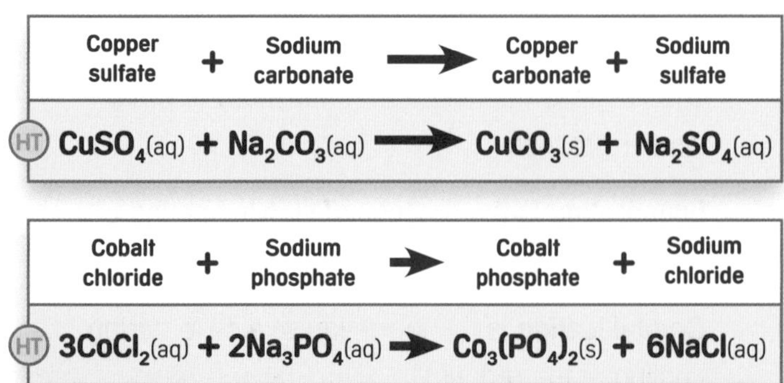

Copper sulfate	+	Sodium carbonate	→	Copper carbonate	+	Sodium sulfate
HT $CuSO_4(aq)$	+	$Na_2CO_3(aq)$	→	$CuCO_3(s)$	+	$Na_2SO_4(aq)$

Cobalt chloride	+	Sodium phosphate	→	Cobalt phosphate	+	Sodium chloride
HT $3CoCl_2(aq)$	+	$2Na_3PO_4(aq)$	→	$Co_3(PO_4)_2(s)$	+	$6NaCl(aq)$

HT It's possible to predict chemicals that can be made by precipitation by looking at how soluble they are in water.

For example...

- all potassium and sodium salts are soluble
- all chlorides are soluble
- almost all oxides, hydroxides and carbonates (potassium and sodium are exceptions) are insoluble.

Key Words Salt • Precipitate • Filtration • Filtrate

Making Soluble Salts

Soluble salts can be made in two different ways. The first method of making a soluble salt is by reacting an **insoluble chemical** with an **acid** in solution.

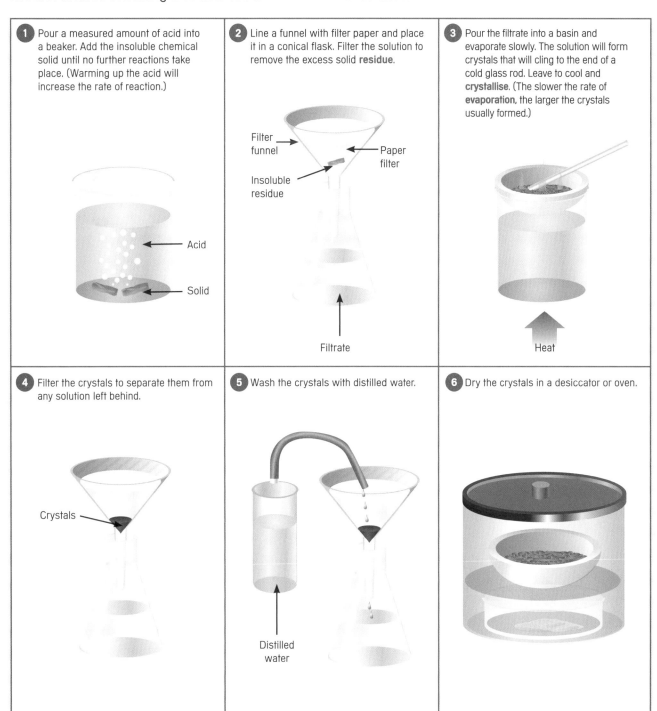

1. Pour a measured amount of acid into a beaker. Add the insoluble chemical solid until no further reactions take place. (Warming up the acid will increase the rate of reaction.)

   Acid
   Solid

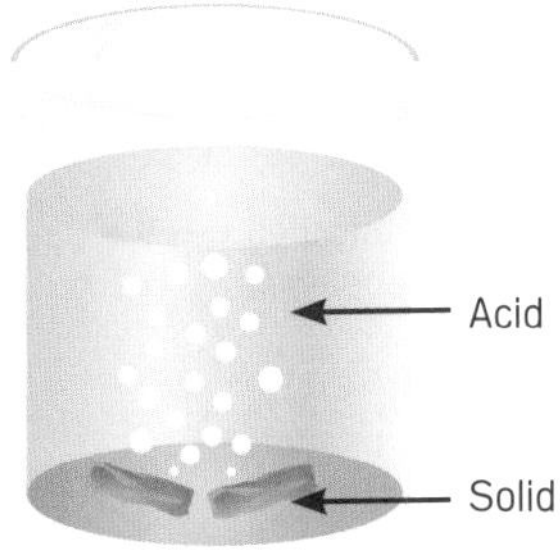

2. Line a funnel with filter paper and place it in a conical flask. Filter the solution to remove the excess solid **residue**.

   Filter funnel
   Paper filter
   Insoluble residue
   Filtrate

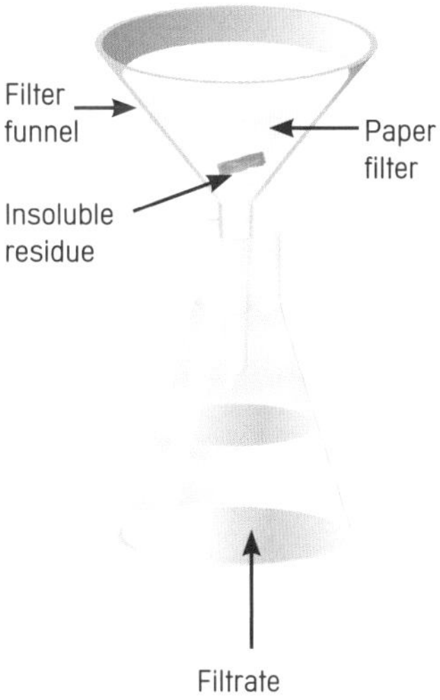

3. Pour the filtrate into a basin and evaporate slowly. The solution will form crystals that will cling to the end of a cold glass rod. Leave to cool and **crystallise**. (The slower the rate of **evaporation**, the larger the crystals usually formed.)

   Heat

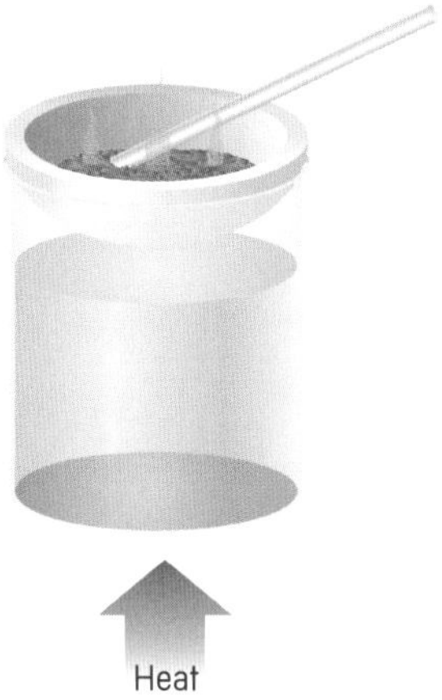

4. Filter the crystals to separate them from any solution left behind.

   Crystals

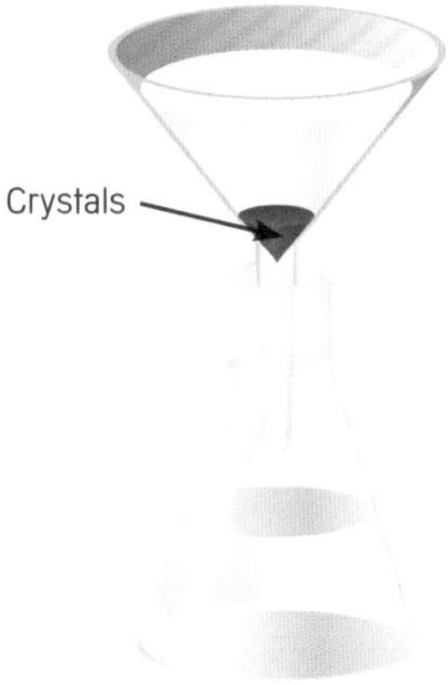

5. Wash the crystals with distilled water.

   Distilled water

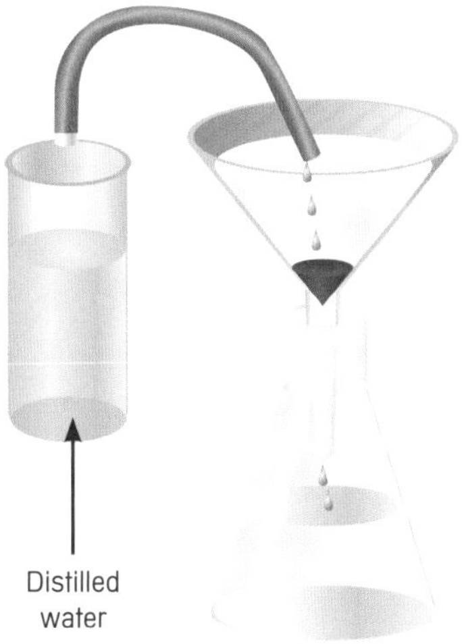

6. Dry the crystals in a desiccator or oven.

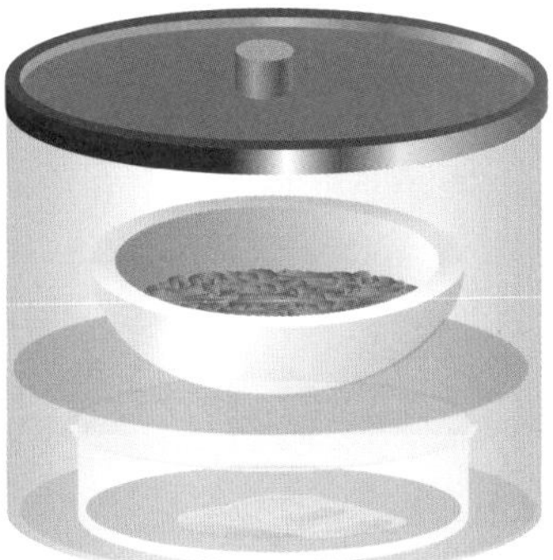

An example of a soluble salt that can be made by reacting an insoluble chemical with an acid is copper sulfate. The symbol and word equations are:

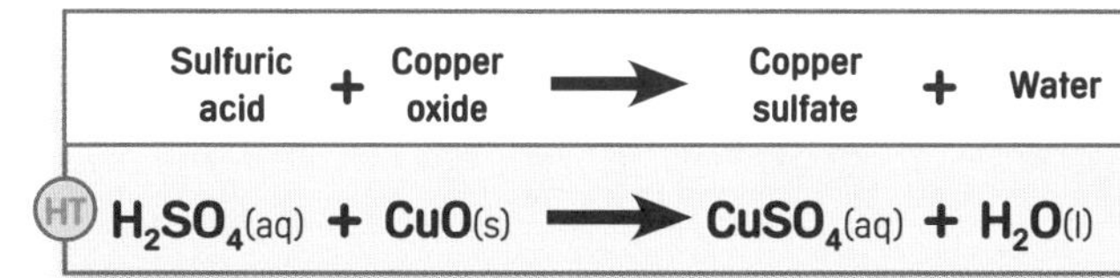
Sulfuric acid + Copper oxide → Copper sulfate + Water
HT $H_2SO_4(aq) + CuO(s) \rightarrow CuSO_4(aq) + H_2O(l)$

Making Soluble Salts (Cont.)

The second method of making **soluble salts** involves **titration**. Titration is a method used to measure the concentration of an **acid** by finding out how much **alkali** is needed to **neutralise** it. When the two solutions have fully reacted, a soluble salt can be formed by **crystallisation**.

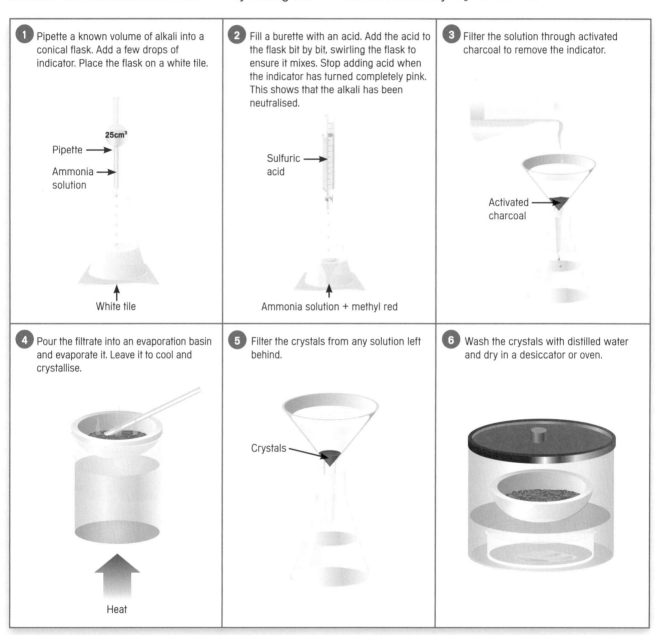

1 Pipette a known volume of alkali into a conical flask. Add a few drops of indicator. Place the flask on a white tile. 25cm³ Pipette Ammonia solution White tile	2 Fill a burette with an acid. Add the acid to the flask bit by bit, swirling the flask to ensure it mixes. Stop adding acid when the indicator has turned completely pink. This shows that the alkali has been neutralised. Sulfuric acid Ammonia solution + methyl red	3 Filter the solution through activated charcoal to remove the indicator. Activated charcoal
4 Pour the filtrate into an evaporation basin and evaporate it. Leave it to cool and crystallise. Heat	5 Filter the crystals from any solution left behind. Crystals	6 Wash the crystals with distilled water and dry in a desiccator or oven.

The indicator allows you to **monitor** the reaction. You should record how much alkali was required to completely neutralise the acid.

Instead of indicator, you could use a pH meter to show when the acid is neutralised.

An example of a soluble salt that can be made by neutralising an acid with an alkali is ammonium sulfate:

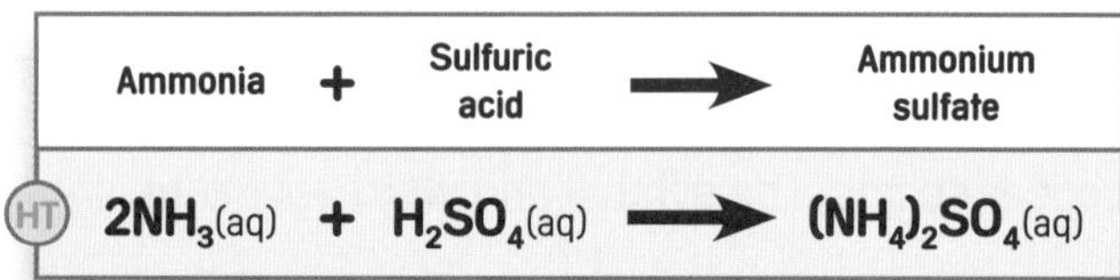

Ammonia	+	Sulfuric acid	→	Ammonium sulfate
HT $2NH_3(aq)$	+	$H_2SO_4(aq)$	→	$(NH_4)_2SO_4(aq)$

 Key Words Soluble • Titration • Acid • Alkali • Neutralise • Crystallisation

Yield

When choosing the best method to manufacture a chemical, scientists look at...

- obtaining the maximum **yield** – the amount of product made in a chemical reaction
- costs
- energy requirements
- how to dispose of or recycle any side products.

The amount of product made in a chemical reaction is known as the **yield**.

Calculating the yield shows how efficient a reaction has been.

The **percentage yield** is calculated by comparing...

- **actual yield** – the amount of product made
- **theoretical yield** – the amount of product expected to be made.

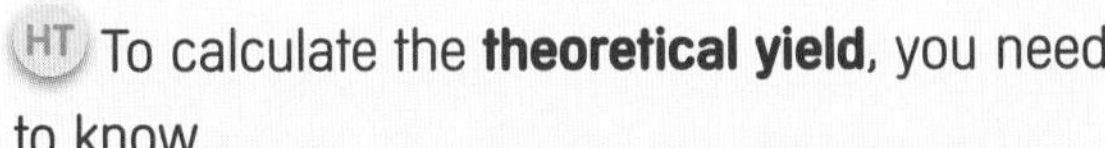

$$\text{Percentage yield} = \frac{\text{Actual yield}}{\text{Theoretical yield}} \times 100$$

HT To calculate the **theoretical yield**, you need to know...

- the chemical equation
- the **relative formula masses** (***M_r***).

For example, to calculate the theoretical yield of copper sulfate produced by 10g sulfuric acid you would work out the following:

Equation: $CuO + H_2SO_4 \longrightarrow CuSO_4 + H_2O$

M_r : 80 + 98 $\longrightarrow$ 160 + 18

So, when 98g of acid is used, 160g of copper sulfate is produced. (The CuO is added in excess and can be ignored.)

Therefore, 10g of acid gives a theoretical yield of...

$\frac{160}{98} \times 10 =$ **16.3g** of copper sulfate.

Quick Test

1. When preparing to filter an insoluble salt that you have prepared, why is the precipitate washed?
2. Give **two** ways of preparing a soluble salt.
3. How would you obtain a dry sample of a soluble salt made in a chemical reaction?
4. Give **two** ways of monitoring a reaction during a titration.
5. What is the amount of product made in a chemical reaction called?

Key Words Yield

B4 Making Chemical Products

Rates of Reactions

Chemical reactions only occur when particles collide with each other with sufficient energy. The more frequent these collisions are, the faster the **rate of reaction**.

There are three factors that affect the rate of reaction:

- The temperature of the reaction mixture.
- The concentration of a solution of the soluble chemical.
- The particle size of an insoluble chemical.

Low Temperature	High Temperature
Slower reaction rate as there are fewer successful collisions in a given period of time. This is because the particles... • move slowly • collide less often and with less energy.	Faster reaction rate as there are more successful collisions in a given period of time. This is because the particles... • move quickly • collide more often and with greater energy.

Low Concentration	High Concentration
Slower reaction rate as there are fewer successful collisions in a given period of time. This is because the particles... • are fewer in number and are spread out • collide less often.	Faster reaction rate as there are more successful collisions in a given period of time. This is because the particles... • are greater in number and are crowded much closer together • collide more often.

Measuring the Rate of Reaction

The rate of a chemical reaction is the amount of reaction that takes place in a given unit of time. You can follow the rate of a chemical reaction in the following ways:

1. If one of the products is a gas, the mass of the mixture will decrease as the gas is produced. Therefore, you can weigh the reaction mixture at timed intervals.
2. If one of the products is a gas, you can collect and measure the volume of gas produced at timed intervals.
3. You can observe the formation of a precipitate. You can do this by...
   - putting a piece of paper marked with a cross underneath the flask containing the reaction and watching to see when the cross is no longer visible
   - measuring the formation of a precipitate or a colour change using a light sensor.
4. It may be possible to measure how quickly one of the reactants disappears.

Key Words Rate of reaction

Catalysts

Almost all industrial chemical reactions use **catalysts**.

A catalyst is a chemical used to speed up the rate of the chemical reaction. A catalyst is unchanged chemically, or in quantity, at the end of the reaction. So, catalysts can be used in small quantities and over and over again.

Examples:

- An iron catalyst is used in the manufacture of ammonia.
- A vanadium(V) oxide catalyst is used in the manufacture of sulfuric acid.

Chemical Production Plants

Chemical production plants are often sited where...

- there is a plentiful supply of chemicals for the reactions
- transport links are good for distribution of the product.

Quick Test

1. Write down **three** factors that affect the rate of a chemical reaction.
2. Explain the term 'catalyst'.
3. Write down **three** ways in which the rate of a chemical reaction can be followed.

Key Words Catalyst

B4 Making Chemical Products

Formulations

Mixing ingredients according to a fixed formula is called **formulation**.

For example, to make a 100cm^3 copper sulfate solution using 5g of copper sulfate to a concentration of 0.05g/cm^3, you would take the following steps:

1. Weigh out 5g of copper sulfate in a beaker.
2. Transfer the solid copper sulfate into a volumetric flask using a funnel.
3. Wash the funnel and beaker with distilled water. Pour the washings into the volumetric flask.
4. Add distilled water to the flask until it's about three-quarters full. Place the stopper in the top and gently shake until all the solid is dissolved.
5. Place the flask on a level surface and add distilled water until the level of the solution reaches the 100cm^3 mark.

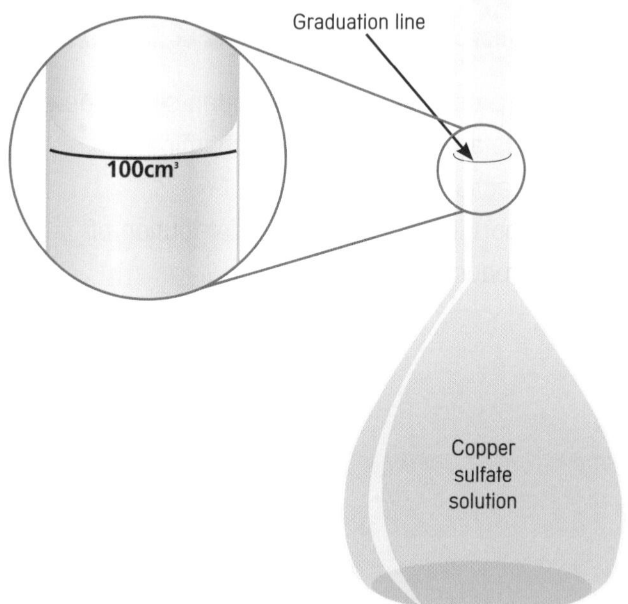

You can adapt the above method to prepare other solutions of a specified concentration.

Concentration can be expressed in...

- grams per litre (g/litre)
- grams per cubic centimetre (g/cm^3)

N.B. 1ml = 1cm^3; 1 litre = 1000ml.

If you know the concentration and volume of a solution, you can calculate the mass of the solute using the following formula:

$$\text{Mass (g)} = \text{Concentration (g/litre or g/cm}^3\text{)} \times \text{Volume (litre or cm}^3\text{)}$$

Quality Control

The effectiveness of chemicals, both pure and synthetic, is tested as part of the quality-control process.

Product formulations undergo tests to ensure...

- quality assurance
- consumer protection
- conformity to national and international standards.

Different companies and countries may use different methods of testing chemicals.

National and international standards have been put in place to guarantee that consistent levels of quality are met.

Making Emulsions and Suspensions

Many food products, drinks, paints, cosmetics and medicines are made of one substance dispersed in another.

An **emulsion** consists of one *liquid* finely dispersed in another *liquid*. Examples include mayonnaise (oil in water) and liquid soaps. Emulsions are useful as their properties are different from their ingredients.

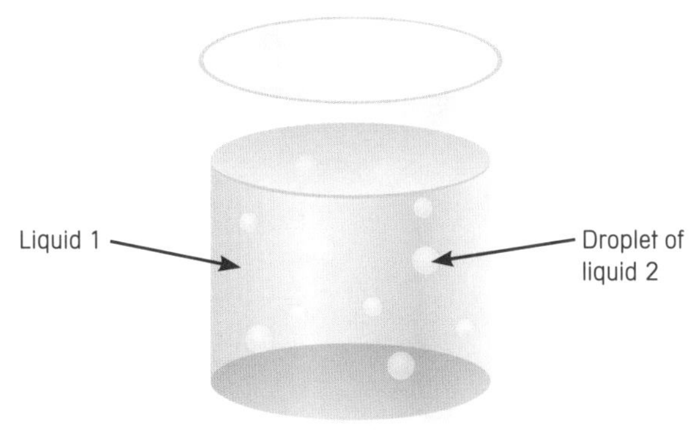

A **suspension** consists of a *solid* dispersed in a *liquid*. Examples include water-based ink and water-based paint.

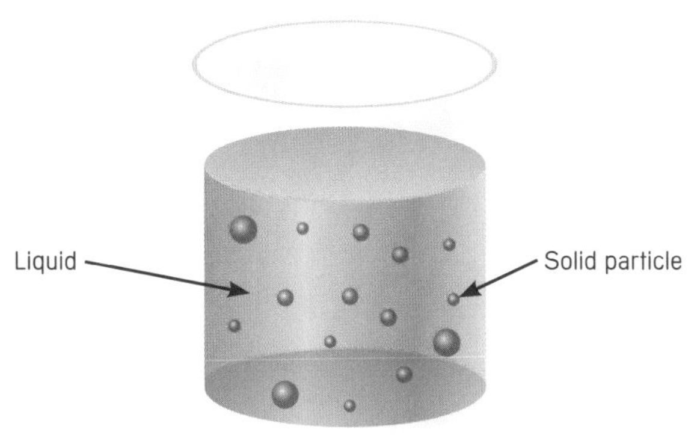

Emulsifying agents can be used to help form emulsions. They stop two liquids that **don't** usually mix from separating.

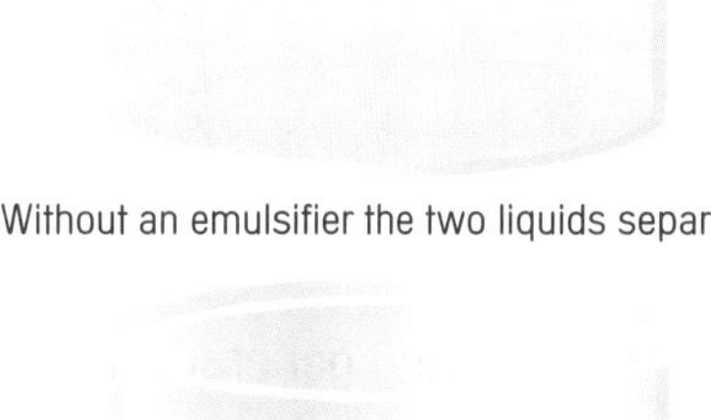

Without an emulsifier the two liquids separate.

With an emulsifying agent a stable emulsion is formed.

HT Emulsions

Emulsions look different to their ingredients because the fine droplets dispersed through them scatter light.

Examples:

- Mayonnaise is an emulsion of oil and vinegar (or lemon juice), with egg yolk as the emulsifier.
- Milk is an emulsion of fat droplets dispersed in a solution of sugars and proteins.

Quick Test

1. A solution contains 180g of a chemical per litre. How much of the chemical would be present in 5 litres of the solution?
2. Give one example of…
   (a) a suspension
   (b) an emulsion.
3. What chemical would you use to help two liquids form an emulsion?

Key Words Emulsion • Suspension • Emulsifying agent

B4 Exam Practice Questions

1 Complete the following definitions. Use words from this list. **[4]**

acid **alkali** **filtrate** **precipitate** **residue** **solute** **yield**

A .... is a solid substance that can be dissolved, making a solution.

The .... is the amount of product that is obtained from a chemical reaction.

An .... is a chemical with a pH of less than 7.

A .... is a solid that is produced as a result of the chemical reaction between two soluble salts.

A .... is a clear liquid that is collected when separating a solid from a liquid.

An .... is a chemical with a pH of more than 7.

When a liquid containing a solid is filtered, the .... is left in the filter paper.

2 Complete the following general acid reactions.

(a) Acid + Metal hydroxide ⟶ .... + ... **[1]**

(b) Acid + Metal carbonate ⟶ .... + ... + ... **[1]**

(c) Acid + Metal ⟶ .... + ... **[1]**

(d) Acid + Metal oxide ⟶ .... + ... **[1]**

3 293g of lead sulfate is obtained from the reaction of lead nitrate and sulfuric acid. The theoretical yield is 303g. What is the percentage yield of the reaction? **[2]**

....

....

4 What are the symbols for the following chemical elements?

(a) Calcium .... **[1]**

(b) Potassium .... **[1]**

(c) Sodium .... **[1]**

(d) Sulfur .... **[1]**

5 25cm^3 of a solution of copper sulfate contains 3g of copper sulfate. Calculate its concentration in g/cm^3. **[2]**

....

....

6 Complete the following sentences. **[2]**

An emulsion is a .... dispersed in a ....

A suspension is a .... dispersed in a ....

7 Describe how to make large crystals of magnesium sulfate.

The quality of written communication will be assessed in your answer to this question. **[6]**

HT 8 Copper oxide and sulfuric acid react together to produce copper sulfate and water. Below is the balanced symbol equation for this reaction:

$$CuO_{(s)} + H_2SO_{4(aq)} \rightarrow CuSO_{4(aq)} + H_2O_{(l)}$$

(A_rs: Cu = 63, O = 16, H = 1, S = 32)

(a) Work out the relative formula mass (M_r) for each of the reactants and products in the equation. **[4]**

(i) CuO ......

(ii) H_2SO_4 ......

(iii) $CuSO_4$ ......

(iv) H_2O ......

(b) Predict the mass of copper sulfate, $CuSO_4$, that will be produced if 15.8g of copper oxide reacts with the sulfuric acid. **[2]**

9 Draw straight lines to join the formulae to the correct compounds. **[3]**

Formulae	Compounds
KOH	Calcium oxide
Na_2SO_4	Potassium hydroxide
$ZnSO_4$	Zinc sulfate
CaO	Sodium sulfate

Answers

Topic A1: Sport and Fitness

Quick Test Answers

Page 7

1. $\text{BMI} = \frac{\text{Body mass in kg}}{(\text{Height in m})^2}$
2. Remove waste; Control the balance of water and other chemicals
3. They dilate to increase heat loss (through the surface of the skin).

Page 9

1. Intercostal muscles
2. **(a)** To carry oxygen in the blood and deliver it to the body's cells.
   (b) Plasma; White blood cells; Platelets
3. The ventricles

Page 11

1. They have thick elastic walls.
2. They contain valves (to prevent backflow of blood).
3. **Any two from:** Support, Protection, To enable movement
4. Ligament
5. Tendon
6. False

Page 13

1. 60 ÷ 1.5 = 40m/s
2. **Any two from:** Anabolic steroids; Human growth hormone; Stimulants; Erythropoietin
3. Treatment of skeletal-muscular injuries
4. Assess progress; Determine trends

Exam Practice Answers

Pages 14–15

1. Lifestyle — Claire goes swimming every day.
   Health — Claire smokes 10 cigarettes a day.
   Fitness — Claire is recovering from flu.
   [1 mark for each correct line up to a maximum of 2.]
2. Count the number of beats for 60 seconds **and** Press firmly with your index and middle finger on the artery in your wrist or arm **should be ticked**.
3. **(a)** (Clinical, electronic sensor or liquid crystal) thermometer
   (b) Sphygmomanometer
4. **(a)** $90 \div 1.78^2 = 28.4$ **[1 mark for correct working but wrong answer]**
   (b) Normal BMI is 18.5–25. Astra is overweight.
5. **A** Right atrium; **B** Left valves; **C** Left ventricle
6. **(a)** **A** Platelets; **B** Plasma; **C** White blood cells; **D** Red blood cells
   (b) **A** Clotting of the blood
   B Carries dissolved substances (food, hormones, waste)
   C Defends the body against disease
   D Collects and delivers oxygen to the cells
7. 800 ÷ 494 = 1.62m/s **[1 mark for correct working but wrong answer]**
8. trachea; diaphragm; ribs; alveoli
9. **This is a model answer which would score full marks**: The intercostal muscles contract, so that the ribs move upwards and outwards. The diaphragm flattens so the volume of the thorax increases. With the increase in volume, air rushes into the lungs. Gases are exchanged across the walls/surface of the alveoli.
10. To avoid risk of injury to the client; To avoid the risk of litigation against the practitioner

Topic A2: Health Care

Quick Test Answers

Page 19

1. Triage
2. **Any two from:** Symptoms; Current medication; Alcohol consumption; Tobacco use; Level of physical activity; Family medical history; Previous treatments
3. **Any two from:** Obesity; Depression; Problems with sleeping; Problems with concentration
4. **Any two from:** To help with diagnosis of a current health problem; To tell the doctor about allergies or serious medical conditions; To make information available to other practitioners so that they can treat the patient if their regular practitioner is unavailable; To keep a record of all medical treatment the patient has received in the past; To allow an investigation if something goes wrong

Page 21

1. In the fallopian tubes
2. To cause the lining of the uterus to repair and thicken (following a period)
3. Uterus (womb)
4. **Any two from:** To explore the fertility problem; To prepare the couple for the success or failure of the treatment; To provide emotional support
5. Five days (after successful fertilisation)
6. Pregnancy test; Ultrasound scan

Page 23

1. Amniotic fluid and the foetus
2. To deliver food and oxygen to the foetus; To remove waste from the foetus
3. Blood vessels
4. Too little insulin in the mother's blood

Page 25

1. The skin is wiped with an antiseptic; A sterile syringe/needle is used.
2. APGAR score
3. **Any three from:** Baby's weight; Length; Reflexes; Motor skills; Response to light and sound; Skin condition

Exam Practice Answers

Pages 26–27

1. Makes health care available to all; Provides specialist care
2. **A** Uterus; **B** Ovary; **C** Fallopian tube
3. **(a)** During pregnancy to monitor the development of the baby
   (b) After birth to monitor the growth of the child
   (c) In A&E departments to prioritise the treatment of patients
   (d) Before undergoing treatment the patient must sign to agree to the treatment to acknowledge rights involved
4. **(a)** Hormone treatment **should be ticked**
   (b) More than one embryo may be placed in the uterus.
5. Amniotic fluid — Where fertilisation occurs
   Fallopian tube — Absorbs shock and stops the baby from getting bumped
   Placenta — Expands to accommodate the foetus during development
   Uterus — Delivers food and oxygen to the foetus
   [1 mark for each correct line up to a maximum of 3.]

Topic A2: Health Care (Cont.)

6.

Name of Condition During Pregnancy	Test	Evidence Leading to Diagnosis
Gestational diabetes	**Glucose tolerance test OR Blood test**	**Glucose is present in the mother's urine.**
Pre-eclampsia	**Blood pressure measurement OR Urine test**	**Mother's blood pressure is high/raised. OR Protein is present in the mother's urine.**

7. It assesses the health of the newborn baby **[1]** to see if the baby has any immediate problems that need support **[1]**.
8. **This is a model answer which would score full marks**: Personal medical information must be recorded, stored and made available to other practitioners so that they know the patient's medical history. Without this information, it would be difficult to treat them, because the patient might have allergies or other serious medical conditions. If things go wrong with the treatment, information in the medical records can be checked, and legal action can be taken if the treatment was not appropriate for that patient. Information in medical records also allows medical practitioners to review the effectiveness (or not) of medical practices used in the treatment of certain conditions.

Topic A3: Monitoring and Protecting the Environment

Quick Test Answers

Page 29

1. To show that evidence from these labs is accepted (as accurate and reliable)
2. Adherence to health and safety regulations; Continual staff development; Regular maintenance and checking of equipment and instruments
3. A test carried out by a number of labs to check the accuracy of their analytical procedures
4. To prevent contamination; To prevent tampering

Page 31

1. **Any three from:** Written descriptions; Drawings; Photographs; Videos
2. The extent to which an object or objects at different distances from the camera are in focus
3. Sampling of ocean organisms shows the organisms that live in a particular area and how the distribution of these may change over a period of time as a result of climate change.
4. An organism whose presence indicates how polluted water is

Page 33

1. 250 × 120 = 30 000m^2
2. Random; Systematic
3. **Any one from:** Imprecise; Not precise
4. Area is calculated from two measurements, each with a degree of uncertainty

Page 35

1. Red
2. **(a)** Qualitative
   (b) Semi-quantitative
3. Dissolved solids exist as ions or molecules in solution. Suspended solids are particles of a similar density to the liquid, spread throughout the liquid.
4. **Any one from:** Turbidity tube; Turbidity meter; Secchi disc

Exam Practice Answers

Pages 36–37

1. accreditation; proficiency
2. | | |
   |---|---|
   | Written description | A rough plan of an area marking sampling points |
   | Drawing | The number and types of butterfly that visit different flowers over a week |
   | Photographs | The feeding behaviour of a bird |
   | Videos | The effects of an oil spill on rock pools |

   [1 mark for each correct line up to a maximum of 3.]
3. | | |
   |---|---|
   | Contrast | Whether the image is blurred or not |
   | Depth of field | A measure of how much bigger the image is than the object |
   | Magnification | The extent to which objects at different distances from the camera are in focus |
   | Sharpness of focus | The extent to which parts of an image are distinguishable from other objects and the background |

   [1 mark for each correct line up to a maximum of 3.]
4. **(a)** The cloudiness resulting from suspended solids
   (b) Any one method from:
   Turbidity tube [1]
   1 Slowly add the water to be tested **[1]**.
   2 Continue to pour the water until the circle just disappears **[1]**.
   3 Take a reading **[1]**.
   Turbidity meter [1]
   1 Place the water sample in the turbidity meter **[1]**.
   2 Switch on. A light is shone through the sample **[1]**.
   3 Take a reading **[1]**.
   Secchi disc [1]
   1 Lower the disc into the water **[1]** until it can't be seen **[1]**.
   2 Record the depth (in metres) **[1]**.
5. **This is a model answer which would score full marks**: Scientists sample organisms in the ocean to identify changes in the species present and changes in their distribution that result from climate change. This distribution is important to investigate, because as oceans are warming up, organisms that live in colder water are moving northwards, and species that live in northern waters may become extinct. This movement of organisms will affect ocean food chains if sources of food move, and also populations of birds that feed on these ocean organisms.

Answers

Topic A3: Monitoring and Protecting the Environment (Cont.)

6.

	Definition	One Possible Cause
Random Error	**Over a number of measurements, values vary in an unpredictable way.**	**Any one from: Low sensitivity of equipment; It's difficult to make measurements.**
Systematic Error	**The values measured are different from the true value in a consistent way, either consistently higher or consistently lower.**	**Any one from: An incorrectly calibrated instrument; The operator making measurements that are consistently incorrect.**

7. Accuracy – How close a measurement is to its true value
Error – The difference between the measured value and its true value
Precision – How closely a number of measurements agree

Topic A4: Scientists Protecting the Public

Quick Test Answers
Page 39
1. True
2. Record, collect and package evidence found at crime scenes
3. Colorimeter
4. Calibration graph

Page 41
1. ×400
2. To hold the slide
3. To see greater surface detail
4. The ability to distinguish separate points of an image
5. A light microscope has a narrow depth of field. An SEM has a wide depth of field.

Page 43
1. Solvent
2. **Any two from:** TLC plates are easier to handle; TLC gives faster runs; More even movement of the mobile phase; A choice of stationary phases; Better results; More easily reproduced results
3. Reference standard
4. The chromatogram is developed.
5. $R_f = \frac{\text{Distance travelled by substance}}{\text{Distance travelled by solvent}}$
6. How strongly the molecules of the substance are attracted to the molecules in the stationary phase and the molecules in the solvent

Page 45
1. (Gel) electrophoresis
2. **Any one from:** To help solve crimes; In paternity testing
3. A database on which people's DNA profiles are stored
4. It amplifies the DNA so that profiles can be produced from very small samples
5. Positive

Exam Practice Answers
Pages 46–47
1. standard, concentration, solution **[1]**; absorbance, transmission **[1]**, calibration **[1]**

2.

Microscopy	Advantages	Disadvantages
Light microscopy	**Any two from: Cheap; Portable; Samples can be prepared quickly; Can observe living specimens**	**Relatively low resolution Relatively low magnification**
Electron microscopy	**High magnification High resolution**	**Any two from: Expensive to buy and run; Living organisms, cells or tissues have to be killed to be observed; Large and static; Samples take a long time to prepare**

3. **(a)** Paper/Thin layer chromatography – will separate the dyes in the mixture so that an identification may be made.
(b) Electrophoresis – DNA can be extracted from the blood. By profiling the DNA it's easy to identify whether the blood is from the victim or the suspect.
(c) Light microscopy – will magnify the hair enough to be able to determine whether the hair still retains the follicle (complete if shed, damaged if pulled, not present in cut hair).
4. **(a)** The solvent that's used to move the substances on the chromatogram.
(b) The medium that the sample is placed on, and through which the sample and mobile phase move.
(c) A chemical used to reveal the presence and position of colourless substances on the chromatogram.
5. **This is a model answer which would score full marks**: Profiling of DNA found at a crime scene can help to identify people who were at that crime scene. It is now possible to use the polymerase chain reaction (PCR) to produce many identical copies of DNA at the crime scene. This makes it possible to produce profiles from tiny amounts of DNA, including DNA from evidence that's been stored for many years. DNA profiles produced can then be compared to check for a match with profiles on the National DNA Database, of people connected with crimes.
6. Higher magnifications are possible with a scanning electron microscope **[1]**. The resolution (the ability to distinguish between two points) is also greater **[1]**.

Topic B1: Sports Equipment

Quick Test Answers

Page 49

1. **Any two from:** British Standards Institution (BSI); European Committee for Standardization; International Organization for Standardization
2. Durable
3. Traceability

Page 53

1. Thermal conductivity
2. **Any three from:** Good conductors of heat and electricity; Shiny; Stiff; Ductile; Malleable
3. Ceramic
4. Can be drawn into a wire
5. It doesn't return to its original shape after a force applied to it is removed.
6. A graph of extension over force is a straight line when showing elastic behaviour. It changes shape, rising steeply as the behaviour becomes plastic.

Page 55

1. A material made from more than one material (usually one material embedded in another)
2. By mixing molten metal with other elements. The elements in the mixture dissolve. When the mixture cools it forms a solid.
3. True

Exam Practice Answers

Pages 56–57

1. **(a)** Kitemark
   (b) CE Mark
2. Brittle **and** Insulators of heat and electricity **should be ticked.**
3. **(a)** How much force is needed to break a material when loaded under tension
   (b) How much force a material can withstand before fracturing when loaded under compression
4. Increasing the thickness of the material; Using stronger or stiffer materials; Changing the structure.
5. 1 Support the material to be tested with a clamp at each end.
   2 Gradually add masses onto the middle of the material.
   3 Record the mass needed to produce a fixed amount of bending.
   4 Repeat the test with different materials. (They must all have the same dimensions.)
   5 The material that needs the greatest mass to make it bend the fixed amount is the stiffest.
6. Because of their thermal conductivity **[1]**. When you touch a material with a high thermal conductivity **[1]**, the heat from your hand easily passes through the material so it feels cold **[1]**.
7. | | |
   |---|---|
   | Stiffness | The resistance of a material to wear |
   | Tensile strength | The resistance of a material to bending |
   | Durability | How resistant a material is to snapping |
   | Toughness | How much force is needed to break a material when stretched |

   [1 mark for each correct line up to a maximum of 3.]
8. **Any three from:** Properties; Cost; Durability; Environmental impact; Appearance
9. **(a)** How a material stretches when it's under tensile stress
   (b) Extension = $\frac{4N}{50N/m}$ = 0.08m (= 8cm)
   [1 mark for correct working but wrong answer]
10. A material showing elastic behaviour will spring back to its original shape when a force is removed **[1]**. A material showing plastic behaviour will not return to its original shape (because the force is too great) **[1]**.
11. **This is a model answer which would score full marks**:
    Composites combine the useful properties of two (or more) different materials while avoiding the drawbacks or weaknesses of the individual materials. For instance, fibreglass is a composite of glass fibres in a resin matrix. **[You could use a labelled diagram to illustrate this.]** The glass provides stiffness to the fibreglass (but is brittle). The resin makes fibreglass tough and gives it a low density / makes it lightweight.
    Or
    For instance, Kevlar® is a polymer used in many composite materials. It's used to add strength, toughness and durability to the composite. It's often combined with carbon-fibre and graphite, which have low density but are less strong, in tennis rackets. In cycling helmets, it's combined with lower density polymers to add strength.

Topic B2: Stage and Screen

Quick Test Answers

Page 59

1. Sunlight
2. A piece of glass or plastic that alters the colour of a light source by absorbing some colours
3. Blue; Green; Red
4. Green

Page 62

1. Transparent
2. Allows light to pass through it but details can't be seen
3. **(a)** Real (or sometimes virtual, e.g. a magnifying glass)
   (b) Virtual
4. Convex
5. **Any three from:** Lens; Shutter; Aperture; Film/image sensor/focal plane; Viewfinder
6. To what extent the material bends (refracts) light (rays)

Page 64

1. 2000Hz (2kHz)
2. Large amplitude
3. **Any one from:** Positioning the speakers in front of the microphone; Pointing the speakers away from the microphone; Placing the microphone close to the performer
4. To keep sounds from the venue in and sounds from the neighbourhood out

Page 67

1. **Any one from:** If one bulb burns out, the other stays lit; The bulbs are not dimmed when additional ones are added; Bulbs can be switched on and off separately
2. Variable resistor
3. **Any two from:** Lighting; Audience; Heating system
4. **Any three from:** Emergency lighting; Emergency exits with clear signage; Fireproof safety curtain; Fire doors

Exam Practice Answers

Pages 68–69

1. **Any three from:** Sunlight; Incandescent lamps; Fluorescent lamps; Lasers
2. incandescent; heating; skin cancer

Answers

Topic B2: Stage and Screen (Cont.)

3.

Colour of Filter	Colour of Light Absorbed	Colour of Light that Appears
Blue	**Red and green**	**Blue**
Red	Blue and green	**Red**
Cyan	**Red**	Cyan

[1 mark for each correct row]

4. 1 Lens
   2 Aperture
   3 Shutter
   4 Focal plane/film/sensor
   5 Viewfinder
   [1 mark for two correct; 2 marks for three correct; 3 marks for four correct; 4 marks for all correct]
5. pitch; sound intensity; linear; 85
6. | | |
   |---|---|
   | Reflective | A material that lets light pass through virtually unchanged |
   | Refractive | A surface that light bounces off |
   | Translucent | A material that allows light to pass through but scatters it |
   | Transparent | A material that light can't pass through |
   | Opaque | A material that can change the direction of light passing through it |

   [1 mark for each correct line up to maximum of 4.]
7. **(a)** Amplifier **B**; Loudspeaker **C**; Microphone **A**
   [1 mark for each correct up to a maximum of 2.]
   (b) Positioning the speakers in front of the microphone **[1]**, pointing the speakers away from the microphone **[1]** and placing the microphone close to the performer **[1]**
8. **This is a model answer which would score full marks**: Light rays from Jodie are focused on the sensor by the camera lens. As Jodie moves closer, the image of her moves beyond the focal plane of the camera and her image becomes larger. To keep Jodie in focus, Claire refocuses the image by moving the camera lens towards Jodie so that light rays are once more brought to focus on the image sensor.

Topic B3: Agriculture, Biotechnology and Food

Quick Test Answers

Page 71

1. **Any three from:** Growing; Transporting; Processing; Storing; Delivering
2. Environmental health officers; Food technologists; Factory inspectors
3. **Any two from:** Prevent poor food quality; Identify and correct issues; Prevent the sale of a contaminated product

Page 76

1. Breed of cow; Animal husbandry
2. How the animal is cared for.
3. **Any three from:** Good nutrition; Good hygiene and health; Preventing and controlling disease; A good living environment
4. Pasteurisation; UHT

Page 77

1. Yeasts; Bacteria; Viruses
2. Aseptic technique
3. By feeding on them and by contaminating them with their waste products
4. Pathogens

Page 79

1. Lag, log/exponential, stationary, death/senescence
2. Glucose ⟶ Carbon dioxide + Alcohol (+ Energy)
3. Conditions remain ideal so microorganisms can be grown over a long period of time.

Page 81

1. Inserting a gene that produces a useful protein from one organism into another organism
2. **Any one from:** To produce the enzyme chymosin; To produce the active ingredient of rennet
3. To keep the microorganisms in suspension, to distribute the contents evenly and to maintain an even temperature
4. Sensors

Exam Practice Answers

Pages 82–83

1. To protect the public's health and safety; To ensure the welfare of animals; To protect the environment
2. **(a)** **A** Lag phase; **B** Log phase/Exponential phase; **C** Stationary phase; **D** Death phase/Senescence
   (b) Lag phase
   (c) Log phase/Exponential phase
   (d) $2^6 = 64$ **[1 mark for correct working but wrong answer.]**
3. | | |
   |---|---|
   | Yeast | Yoghurt |
   | Bacteria | Bread |
   | | Alcohol |

   [1 mark for both lines from yeast; 1 mark for line from bacteria]
4. **(a)** Glucose + Oxygen ⟶ Carbon dioxide + Water (+ Energy)
   [1 mark for correct reactants; 1 mark for correct products]
   (b) Glucose ⟶ Lactic acid (+ Energy)
   [1 mark for correct reactants; 1 mark for correct products]
5. Batch culture: advantage – easy to set up and maintain; disadvantage – conditions quickly change from the ideal. Continuous culture: advantage – conditions remain ideal throughout; disadvantage – expensive to set up and maintain.

Topic B3: Agriculture, Biotechnology and Food (Cont.)

6. **This is a model answer which would score full marks**: Chemical fertilisers release nutrients quickly into the soil and increase the growth and yield of the crop. But excess fertilisers can be washed by the rain into streams or rivers, which become enriched with nutrients. This process is called eutrophication. There will be a huge growth of algae, removing oxygen from the water/leading to the death of the organisms in the stream or river.

7. **(a)** **(b)**

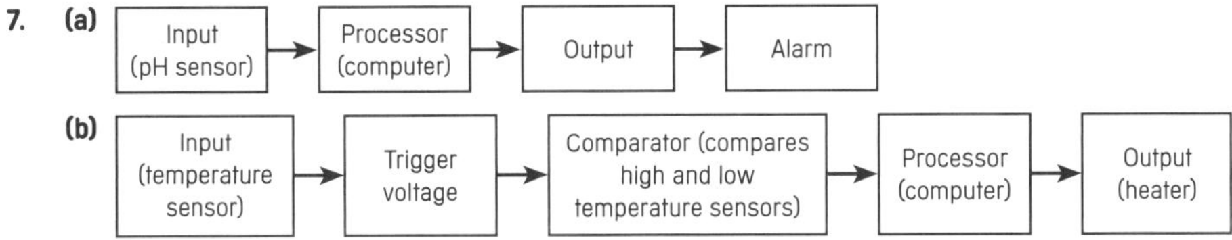

Topic B4: Making Chemical Products

Quick Test Answers

Page 85

1. A chemical made on a large scale
2. **Any one from:** Medicines; Dyes; Pigments
3. **(a)** Electrical wires
   (b) Building construction
4. Technical; Laboratory; Analytical

Page 88

1. **(a)** Nitrogen from the air and hydrogen from natural gas
   (b) Sulfur or sulfur ore, oxygen (from the air) and water
   (c) Salt water

Page 93

1. To remove unreacted chemicals and the other (soluble) chemical product
2. Reacting an insoluble chemical with an acid; Titration
3. By crystallisation (or evaporation)
4. Using indicator; A pH meter
5. Yield

Page 95

1. Particle size (of an insoluble chemical); Concentration (of a soluble chemical); Temperature
2. A chemical that speeds up a chemical reaction but is unchanged in the reaction.
3. **Any three from:** The mass of the reaction mixture (if one of the products is a gas); The volume of gas produced; The rate of formation of the product, e.g. a precipitate; How quickly one of the reactants disappears.

Page 97

1. 900g
2. **(a)** **Any one from:** Water-based ink; Water-based paint
   (b) **Any one from:** Mayonnaise; Liquid soap
3. Emulsifying agent

Exam Practice Answers

Pages 98–99

1. solute; yield; acid; precipitate; filtrate; alkali; residue
   [1 mark if three correct; 2 marks if four correct; 3 marks if five correct; 4 marks if all correct]
2. **(a)** Salt + Water
   (b) Salt + Water + Carbon dioxide
   (c) Salt + Hydrogen
   (d) Salt + Water
3. $\frac{293}{303} \times 100 = 96.7\%$
   [1 mark for correct working but wrong answer.]
4. **(a)** Ca
   (b) K
   (c) Na
   (d) S
5. $\frac{3}{25} = 0.12\text{g/cm}^3$
   [1 mark for correct working but wrong answer.]
6. liquid; liquid; solid; liquid
7. **This is a model answer which would score full marks**: React solid magnesium carbonate with sulfuric acid until the liquid stops fizzing and no more magnesium carbonate will react. Filter the mixture to remove the residue. Collect the filtrate, which is magnesium sulfate solution. Pour the filtrate into an evaporating basin, and allow the water to evaporate slowly so as to form crystals of magnesium sulfate. Filter the crystals off, wash carefully with distilled water, and dry them in a desiccator.
8. **(a)** **(i)** 63 + 16 = 79
   (ii) (2 × 1) + 32 + (4 × 16) = 98
   (iii) 63 + 32 + (4 × 16) = 159
   (iv) (2 × 1) + 16 = 18
   (b) 31.8g $CuSO_4$
   Working out:
   79g of copper oxide will produce 159g of copper sulfate
   15.8g of copper oxide will produce (159/79 × 15.8)g of copper sulfate
   = 31.8g of copper sulfate
   [1 mark for correct working but wrong answer.]
9.

[1 mark for each correct line up to a maximum of 3.]

Glossary of Key Words

Accreditation – recognition of meeting certain criteria

Acid – an aqueous compound with a pH value less than 7

Aerobic respiration – the process that releases energy from food using oxygen; aerobic respiration uses glucose and produces carbon dioxide and water

Alkali – an aqueous compound with a pH value greater than 7

Alloy – a mixture of two or more metals or a mixture of a metal and a non-metal

Alveolus – a tiny air sac in the lungs where gas exchange occurs (Plural: Alveoli)

Amnion (Amniotic sac) – membrane in which a baby develops

Amniotic fluid – watery fluid in which a foetus/baby is suspended in the amnion

Amplitude – the size of a wave, measured from the middle point to the peak (or trough); the amplitude is related to the loudness of a sound

Anaerobic respiration – the process that releases energy from food in the absence of oxygen; using anaerobic respiration, yeast produces alcohol and carbon dioxide from glucose, and Lactobacilli and mammalian muscle produce lactic acid from glucose

Animal husbandry – the care and breeding of animals

Antenatal care – care provided during pregnancy

Aqueous solution – a solution made when a solute dissolves in water

Artery – a vessel that carries blood away from the heart towards the organs

Artificial insemination – introducing sperm artificially into a female animal

Aseptic technique – precautionary measure used by microbiologists to ensure sterile conditions and prevent contamination

Atrium – one of the upper chambers of the heart; the atria receive blood coming back to the heart (Plural: Atria)

Baseline assessment – an initial, basic health/fitness assessment

Batch culture – a closed system culture of microorganisms with specific nutrient types and environmental conditions, produced as a single batch rather than as a continuous process

Bioreactor – a vessel where products from microorganisms are made by fermentation

Biotechnology – any technological application that uses biological systems for a specific use

Blood pressure – the pressure of the blood against the walls of the arteries

Body mass index (BMI) – a calculation that compares a person's mass against his/her height to see if he/she has a healthy weight

Breed – different forms of an animal belonging to the same species

Bronchiole – a small branch of the bronchi

Bronchus – a branch of the trachea (windpipe) (Plural: Bronchi)

Bulk chemical – a chemical made on a large scale

Capillary – a vessel that connects an artery to a vein

Cartilage – reduces friction between moving bones and acts as a shock absorber

Catalyst – a chemical used to speed up the rate of the chemical reaction. The catalyst is unchanged (chemically, or in quantity) at the end of the reaction.

Chain of food production – every stage in the production of food, including growing, transporting, processing, storing and delivery

Chromatography – a technique used to separate unknown mixtures for analysis

Colorimeter – an instrument used to measure the intensity of a colour

Composite material – a material in which one material is embedded into another

Compound – a substance consisting of two or more elements chemically combined

Compressive strength – measures the force a material can withstand before fracturing when loaded under compression

Conductor of electricity – a material that allows electricity to flow through it

Continuous culture – a culture of microorganisms in which the medium is continually replenished with nutrients and environmental conditions remain constant

Contrast – the extent to which parts of an image stand out from other objects and the background

Converging lens – a lens that causes light rays passing through it to meet at a point

Crystallisation – the formation of solid crystals from a solution

Depth of field – the extent to which an object or objects at different distances from the camera are in focus or the extent to which parts of an object viewed with a microscope are in focus

Diagnosis – the decision reached regarding the identification of a condition

Diaphragm – a muscular 'sheet' dividing the thorax and abdomen

Dimmer – a component of a circuit that allows you to adjust the brightness of a light

Diverging lens – a lens that causes light rays passing though it to spread out

DNA – deoxyribonucleic acid; DNA contains the genetic information carried by every cell

Durability – the ability to resist wear and tear

Dye – a soluble chemical used to colour fibres or food

Electron microscope – an instrument that uses a beam of electrons to magnify an object

Electrophoresis – a process that separates charged particles and can be used to identify small biological samples

Element – a chemical that can't be split into simpler substances

Embryo – a ball of cells that will develop into a human/animal baby

Emulsifying agent – an additive that stops two liquids that don't usually mix from separating

Emulsion – a substance that consists of one liquid finely dispersed in another liquid

Environmental health officer – a person who ensures that food we eat is safe through inspection and investigation

Enzyme – a protein that speeds up a chemical reaction

Error – the difference between a measured value and the true value

Evaporation – the process of heating a substance in order to remove water

Factory inspector – inspects food production factories to ensure appropriate procedures are in place

Fermentation – a type of respiration of microorganisms

Fermenter – a vessel where products from microorganisms are made by fermentation

Fertilisation – the fusion of a male nucleus with a female nucleus

Fertiliser – inorganic chemical or organic material applied to plants to increase yield

Filter – a piece of coloured glass or plastic that alters the colour of a light source by absorbing some colours

Filtrate – the clear liquid produced during filtration

Filtration – passing a mixture through a porous material to separate solid particles from a liquid

Fine chemical – a chemical made on a small scale

Fitness – your physical condition; fitness can be improved by exercise and proper nutrition

Focal length – the distance from the lens to the focal plane

Focal plane – a point where images are focused

Food technologist – a person who studies the chemistry, quality and manufacturing process of food

Formula – shows the elements present in a compound and how many there are of each (Plural: Formulae)

Frequency – the number of vibrations produced within a given time period

Glossary of Key Words

Fungicide – a chemical used to prevent disease or death caused by fungi

Gene – made up of DNA; controls the production of a protein

Genetic – determined by genes

Genetic modification – changing the genetic makeup of an organism by introducing genetic information from another organism

Harvest – the collection/gathering of a food crop (or microorganisms)

Health – your physical and mental well-being and whether you have a disease or injury

Heart – a muscular organ that pumps blood around the body

Herbicide – a chemical used to kill unwanted plants (weeds)

Image – a representation of an object

Indicator organism (Indicator species) – an organism whose presence indicates the level of environmental pollution

Infrared radiation – a type of electromagnetic radiation with wavelengths longer than visible light but shorter than radio waves

Insecticide – a chemical used to prevent damage by insect pests

Insoluble – an insoluble substance is one that doesn't dissolve in a solvent

Intercostal muscles – muscles between the ribs, used to raise and lower them

***In-vitro* fertilisation** – a treatment for fertility problems in which fertilisation is done outside the body

Kidney – an organ in the body that filters blood to remove waste and control the balance of water and other chemicals

Lifestyle – your way of living

Ligament – tissue that connects bones together in a joint

Light microscope – an instrument that magnifies a specimen and which uses a beam of light to magnify an object

Lung – an organ that is part of the breathing system

Magnification – the size of the image in relation to the size of the object

Menstrual cycle – monthly cycle of hormonal changes in a woman to prepare the body to carry a baby

Microorganism – a microscopic organism, for example, yeasts, bacteria and viruses

Mobile phase – carries chemicals from a sample through the stationary phase in chromatography

Monitoring – observing or carrying out tests or measurements over a period of time

Muscle – tissue that can contract or be relaxed to produce movement

Neutralise – react an acid and an alkali to form a salt

Oestrogen – a female sex hormone that causes the uterus lining to thicken after a period

Opaque – doesn't let light pass through

Organism – any living thing, e.g. plant, animal, etc.

Parallel circuit – a circuit where the electrical charge can move along more than one path

Pasteurisation – heat treatment used to kill harmful microorganisms in a food product

Pathogen – a disease-causing microorganism

pH – a measure of the acidity or alkalinity of an aqueous solution

pH scale – a scale, ranging from 0–14, used to measure the strength of an acid or alkali

Physiotherapist – a specialist in the treatment of skeletal-muscular injuries

Pigment – an insoluble chemical used to colour paints, food and plastics

Pitch – how high or low a sound is; pitch changes with frequency

Placenta – soft, spongy tissue in the womb which delivers food and oxygen to a developing foetus and removes waste

Platelet – a cell fragment found in blood plasma

Post-natal care – care provided after the birth of a baby

Practitioner – a person with special training to help maintain and improve the health or fitness of others

Precipitate – an insoluble solid formed during a precipitation process

Precipitation – the formation of an insoluble solid when two solutions are mixed

Progesterone – a female sex hormone that prepares the uterus for a fertilised egg

Pulse rate – the number of times a heart beats each minute

Qualitative – a test that relies on visual observation or the results of such a test

Quantitative – a test that measures a given property and gives a numerical value or the results of such a test

Rate of reaction – the amount of reaction that takes place in a given unit of time

Real image – an image that can be focused on a screen

Red blood cell – a type of cell found in blood that transports oxygen from the lungs to the organs

Reflective – a surface that light or sound bounces off

Refraction – a change in direction of light as it crosses the boundary between one material and another

Resazurin – a reagent used to test the freshness of milk

Residue – the substance that remains after a chemical reaction or process (e.g. filtration)

Resistance – a measure of how hard it is for a current to pass through a component at a particular voltage

Resolution – the ability to distinguish between two separate but adjacent points

R_f value – a measure of the movement of a substance relative to the movement of the solvent

Rib – a bone; the ribs protect the contents of the thorax (the region of the chest including the heart and lungs)

Salt – the product of a chemical reaction between an alkali and an acid

Sediment – a layer made of particles that are denser than the liquid they are in; the particles sink to the bottom

Selective breeding – a breeding programme used in animals and plants where those with useful characteristics are bred, while those less suitable are prevented from breeding. The useful characteristics are improved over several generations

Semi-quantitative – gives an approximate quantity or value of a substance in a sample

Series circuit – a circuit where the electrical charge can move along only one path

Sharpness of focus – whether an image seen is sharp or blurred

Side effect – a condition caused by a treatment in addition to its intended effect

Soluble – a soluble solid is one that will dissolve in a solvent to make a solution

Solvent – a substance (liquid) that dissolves another to make a solution

Stationary phase – the medium through which the mobile phase travels in chromatography

Suspended solid – a particle that has a similar density to the liquid it's in, which causes it to disperse throughout it rather than sink or float

Suspension – a substance that consists of a solid dispersed in a liquid

Switch – a component of a circuit that allows current to pass through only when it's pushed or pressed

Symptom – a visible or noticeable effect of a disease, illness or injury

Tendon – tissue that connects a muscle to a bone

Tensile strength – measures the stretching force needed to break a material loaded under tension

Thermal conductivity – a measure of how easily heat flows through a material

Thermal reflectivity – a measure of how easily heat is reflected by a material

Titration – a method used to measure how much of one solution is needed to react exactly with another of known volume

Trachea (windpipe) – the tube that delivers air to and from the lungs

Translucent – lets light pass through but scatters it

Transparent – lets light pass through virtually unchanged

Glossary of Key Words

Turbidity – cloudiness of a liquid caused by suspended solids

UHT – the ultra-high temperature process used to kill all the microorganisms in milk

Ultrasound scan – an imaging technique used to examine babies in the womb

Ultraviolet radiation – a type of electromagnetic radiation with wavelengths shorter than visible light

Umbilical cord – connects a developing foetus/baby to the placenta of its mother and carries blood between the two

Valve – ensures the flow of a liquid (e.g. blood) in the right direction

Vein – a vessel that carries blood from the organs to the heart

Ventricle – one of the lower chambers of the heart; the ventricles pump blood out of the heart

Virtual image – an image that can't be focused on a screen

White blood cell – a type of cell found in blood that defends the body against microorganisms

Yield – the amount of product obtained, e.g. from a crop or a chemical reaction

HT **Accuracy** – how close a measurement is to the true value

Batch process – a process that produces a single batch of a chemical, or a product from a microorganism. To make more of the product, the process has to be repeated

Cloning – producing genetically identical copies of a microorganism, plant or animal

Comparator – a device used to compare sensors

Continuous process – a process that produces a chemical, or a product from a microorganism, continuously. Reactants are fed into the reactor at one end, and the product(s) removed at the other

Drilling – sowing seeds

Elastic behaviour – property of a material that springs back into shape after a force is removed

Hormone – a chemical messenger, part of the communication system

Input – detects energy and converts it to electrical energy. Sensors are input devices

Moment – the turning effect of a force on a lever; it depends on the size of the force and the distance from the fulcrum

Output – converts the electrical energy from a processor into another form of energy that can be used

Plastic behaviour – property of a material that doesn't return to its original shape after a force is removed

Precision – the closeness of agreement between a series of measurements

Processor – changes the electrical energy from the input so that the electronic system can do its job

Receptor – a cell or organ that detects a stimulus

Relative atomic mass (A_r) – the average mass of an atom compared with an atom of carbon

Relative formula mass (M_r) – the sum of the relative atomic masses in a compound, as shown in a chemical formula

Traceability – a chain of regular checking of equipment within laboratories or companies, against national standards and against international standards, to ensure that scientists know the accuracy of measurements they make

Two-way chromatography – a technique used to separate chemicals in a mixture that have similar R_f values; the chromatogram obtained using the first solvent is turned through 90° and placed in a second solvent

Uncertainty – a quantitative indication of the variability of results in an analysis; uncertainty of results arises from random error and systematic error

Key

relative atomic mass **atomic symbol** name atomic (proton) number

1
H
hydrogen
1

1	2											3	4	5	6	7	0
																	4 **He** helium 2
7 **Li** lithium 3	9 **Be** beryllium 4											11 **B** boron 5	12 **C** carbon 6	14 **N** nitrogen 7	16 **O** oxygen 8	19 **F** fluorine 9	20 **Ne** neon 10
23 **Na** sodium 11	24 **Mg** magnesium 12											27 **Al** aluminium 13	28 **Si** silicon 14	31 **P** phosphorus 15	32 **S** sulfur 16	35.5 **Cl** chlorine 17	40 **Ar** argon 18
39 **K** potassium 19	40 **Ca** calcium 20	45 **Sc** scandium 21	48 **Ti** titanium 22	51 **V** vanadium 23	52 **Cr** chromium 24	55 **Mn** manganese 25	56 **Fe** iron 26	59 **Co** cobalt 27	59 **Ni** nickel 28	63.5 **Cu** copper 29	65 **Zn** zinc 30	70 **Ga** gallium 31	73 **Ge** germanium 32	75 **As** arsenic 33	79 **Se** selenium 34	80 **Br** bromine 35	84 **Kr** krypton 36
85 **Rb** rubidium 37	88 **Sr** strontium 38	89 **Y** yttrium 39	91 **Zr** zirconium 40	93 **Nb** niobium 41	96 **Mo** molybdenum 42	[98] **Tc** technetium 43	101 **Ru** ruthenium 44	103 **Rh** rhodium 45	106 **Pd** palladium 46	108 **Ag** silver 47	112 **Cd** cadmium 48	115 **In** indium 49	119 **Sn** tin 50	122 **Sb** antimony 51	128 **Te** tellurium 52	127 **I** iodine 53	131 **Xe** xenon 54
133 **Cs** caesium 55	137 **Ba** barium 56	139 **La*** lanthanum 57	178 **Hf** hafnium 72	181 **Ta** tantalum 73	184 **W** tungsten 74	186 **Re** rhenium 75	190 **Os** osmium 76	192 **Ir** iridium 77	195 **Pt** platinum 78	197 **Au** gold 79	201 **Hg** mercury 80	204 **Tl** thallium 81	207 **Pb** lead 82	209 **Bi** bismuth 83	[209] **Po** polonium 84	[210] **At** astatine 85	[222] **Rn** radon 86
[223] **Fr** francium 87	[226] **Ra** radium 88	[227] **Ac*** actinium 89	[261] **Rf** rutherfordium 104	[262] **Db** dubnium 105	[266] **Sg** seaborgium 106	[264] **Bh** bohrium 107	[277] **Hs** hassium 108	[268] **Mt** meitnerium 109	[271] **Ds** darmstadtium 110	[272] **Rg** roentgenium 111	Elements with atomic numbers 112–116 have been reported but not fully authenticated						

*The lanthanoids (atomic numbers 58–71) and the actinoids (atomic numbers 90–103) have been omitted.
The relative atomic masses of copper and chlorine have not been rounded to the nearest whole number.

Index